'Masterful insight, this book is more relevant th
business leaders of today and tomorrow. Through many illustrations and case studies,
learn how AI is inevitable for your business to boost innovation, efficiency, and for it to
become autonomous!'

Pascal Bornet, *Author of* Intelligent Automation

'The book provides a clear picture of the state of AI in business today and where it is
heading. It inspires innovation and shows how success can be achieved with many
practical examples and detailed case studies. Essential reading for all business
decision-makers ready to embrace the future!'

Dr Adam Bujak, *Co-founder and CEO, KYP.ai*

'Burnett offers a comprehensive foundation and directional understanding of the future
of business in this book. Her years of analyses into the world of technology shines
through, as she explains the current state of artificial intelligence being used across
the world of business and why you should get involved. She weaves a series of exciting
case studies, from a wide range of examples to bring to life a story of potential for
the companies and individuals involved at this evolutionary initial step towards an
autonomous enterprise. A must read.'

Rob Hughes, *Co-founder and CEO, Techopian*

'I recommend this book for executives who need a business-focused primer on AI and
the opportunities that it brings for innovation and efficiency. The book explains AI and
Intelligent Automation as the next set of innovation levers driving business results
in leading enterprises. Executives will learn the language of Intelligent Automation,
including the major classes of tools, their capabilities, and limitations, and how they
work together. Sarah Burnett's book addresses implementation challenges and the
practices that delivered business value in real-world case studies.'

Mary Lacity, *Walton Professor of Information Systems at the University of
Arkansas, Co-author of* Becoming Strategic with Robotic Process Automation

''AI' is the buzzword that business claim to have embedded, but in reality many have
struggled to adapt and underpin their companies with true AI capabilities. In this book,
Sarah Burnett seamlessly makes the concepts and implementation of AI accessible to
all business leaders looking to undertake the digital transformation journeys necessary
for their companies to survive and thrive using the true benefits of AI.'

Russ Shaw CBE, *Founder of Tech London Advocates & Global Tech Advocates*

'Sarah has an ability to simplify the complex. Her approach makes for easy reading and
those real-life examples help to cut through the noise that AI attracts and shine a light
on the real value it delivers. As a serial entrepreneur and investor in AI, I appreciate
the inclusion of case studies that demonstrate the art of the possible and bring this
fascinating technology to life.'

Andrew Anderson, *Serial AI entrepreneur and investor*

THE AUTONOMOUS ENTERPRISE

BCS, THE CHARTERED INSTITUTE FOR IT

BCS, The Chartered Institute for IT, is committed to making IT good for society. We use the power of our network to bring about positive, tangible change. We champion the global IT profession and the interests of individuals, engaged in that profession, for the benefit of all.

Exchanging IT expertise and knowledge
The Institute fosters links between experts from industry, academia and business to promote new thinking, education and knowledge sharing.

Supporting practitioners
Through continuing professional development and a series of respected IT qualifications, the Institute seeks to promote professional practice tuned to the demands of business. It provides practical support and information services to its members and volunteer communities around the world.

Setting standards and frameworks
The Institute collaborates with government, industry and relevant bodies to establish good working practices, codes of conduct, skills frameworks and common standards. It also offers a range of consultancy services to employers to help them adopt best practice.

Become a member
Over 70,000 people including students, teachers, professionals and practitioners enjoy the benefits of BCS membership. These include access to an international community, invitations to a roster of local and national events, career development tools and a quarterly thought-leadership magazine. Visit www.bcs.org/membership to find out more.

Further information
BCS, The Chartered Institute for IT,
3 Newbridge Square,
Swindon, SN1 1BY, United Kingdom.
T +44 (0) 1793 417 417
(Monday to Friday, 09:00 to 17:00 UK time)
www.bcs.org/contact
http://shop.bcs.org/

THE AUTONOMOUS ENTERPRISE
Powered by AI

Sarah Burnett

Published by BCS Learning and Development Ltd, a wholly owned subsidiary of BCS, The Chartered Institute for IT, 3 Newbridge Square, Swindon, SN1 1BY, UK.
www.bcs.org

Paperback ISBN: 978-1-78017-5829
PDF ISBN: 978-1-78017-5836
ePUB ISBN: 978-1-78017-5843

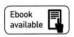

British Cataloguing in Publication Data.
A CIP catalogue record for this book is available at the British Library.

Disclaimer:

Publisher's acknowledgements
Reviewers: Christine Burt and Andrew Lowe
Publisher: Ian Borthwick
Commissioning editor: Rebecca Youé
Production manager: Florence Leroy
Project manager: Sunrise Setting Ltd
Copy-editor: Andrea Ashworth
Proofreader: Barbara Eastman
Indexer: Matthew Gale
Cover design: Alex Wright
Cover image: istock/ngkaki
Typeset by Lapiz Digital Services, Chennai, India
Printed by Hobbs the Printers Ltd, Totton, UK

CONTENTS

LIST OF FIGURES AND TABLES

AUTHOR

Sarah Burnett is a renowned technology industry analyst and international speaker who advises enterprises on intelligent automation, ethical uses of technology, competitive strategies and market trends. She helps intelligent automation technology vendors successfully formulate their product direction, go to market strategies, and apply ethical policies.

She gained her masters degree in applied optics in 1982 from Reading University, and has worked in the computer industry ever since, the last eight of those in the field of intelligent automation.

Sarah is a strong advocate for women in technology. She chaired BCS Women for four years and continues to work with the group as chair of AI Accelerator, which she founded in 2017. AI Accelerator is a programme of free AI events by experts, to inform participants and make AI accessible to more people.

Sarah is a Fellow of BCS.

FOREWORD

'AI' has always been long on rhetoric and striking examples, and short on what is mostly, really, happening in our organisations. For a long time now Sarah Burnett has provided seasoned objective, detailed and valuable insight on automation and digitalisation, and has always been one of the few analysts you go to automatically to find out what is happening, and what is going to happen. This is the long-awaited book. It draws on an impressive knowledge hinterland thoroughly wrung from the author's roles as researcher, practitioner and analyst. She has spent much time engaging with and thinking through myriad examples across sectors and the globe. She has always been incredibly up to date. Unsurprisingly, this is a distinctive feature of the book. An introductory chapter – alone worth the price of the volume – offers a detailed overview explaining the concept of the autonomous enterprise, and many examples spread across retail, finance and healthcare.

The book then gives a very comprehensive and detailed analysis of what 'AI' amounts to. I have always found this a task best compared to hacking one's way through a conceptual jungle full of strange noises and false trails. The author does an outstanding job of making the vocabulary consistent and usable, and the area understandable. With the jungle behind us, there is then relatively sunlit uplands in the form of a compelling assessment, using many illustrations, of how these technologies are already being used to achieve innovation and efficiency, and much more besides.

Reading these chapters it becomes clear that the potential is massive, that imagination and disciplined management are required, and that an enormous amount of value is still being left on the table. Four enlightening case studies follow, and these ground our understanding in the management realities of organisational functioning. Having written a few case studies in my time, I can say that these are exceptional in spelling out the vision needed, the preparatory work, the investment, the organisational challenges and the sheer hard work required.

While many talk of fast digital transformation, and the imminent arrival of digital business, this book posits no overnight successes, rather a slow evolution, with automation at the heart of things. The view of the autonomous enterprise is distinctive and convincing. Automation changes how things are done in the enterprise. For example, it turns traditional knowledge work inside out. Enterprises have to document not only processes but the expertise that they codify to create the automations. Organisations need to prepare for many such possibilities and adapt to ensure success. An autonomous enterprise mindset is required; start with the end in mind, focus on the 'phygital' (it's in the book, dear reader), practice good data stewardship, stay agile and be very aware of how things can go wrong. The book also rightly stresses a collaborative approach and pooling of resources. In my own research I have often found an execution gap opening up between those doing automation and those responsible for digital transformation. New silos for old. But digital transformation, to be successful, as the book makes clear, must converge digital technologies.

The book gets macro in its final chapter, being rightly less pessimistic about job losses and skills, and very clear-eyed about the ethical dimensions of using AI, and indeed all technologies. It's a book to be massively informed by, and it is clearly written, with multiple examples and well digested and analysed empirical research. Like contemporary art, only ten per cent of today's 'AI' literature is really worth engaging with. This is one of those.

Professor Leslie Willcocks
December 2021

Professor Emeritus at London School of Economics and Political Science, Associate Fellow at Green Templeton College Oxford, Research Director at Knowledge Capital Partners, and co-author of four books on automation, including Becoming Strategic with Robotic Process Automation (SB Publishing, 2019).

ACKNOWLEDGEMENTS

This book is the culmination of a 40-year career in IT, eight years of which have been in the field of intelligent automation (IA), focusing on industry analysis and advisory work, with 18 months of specific research. During this time, I had the pleasure of working with many innovative IA software developers and users, to get their perspectives on the wave of change sweeping across enterprises today, as the automation of knowledge work continues apace. There are many people who, over the years, have contributed to the knowledge that I have shared with you. I am grateful to them all. Here, I would like to thank those who have contributed most recently and specifically to this book.

Firstly, I would like to thank my husband, Dr Tim Burnett, for the enormous support that he gave me when I was writing this book and acting as a sounding board for my ideas. Without his constant enthusiasm and encouragement, it would not have been possible.

I am grateful to all the organisations that have shared their practical perspectives with me as users of AI technology. Unfortunately I am unable to name them all except for the few who agreed to share their experience in the named case studies provided in Part 2. I would like to thank the following for their time and the incredibly valuable and practical insights that their case studies have provided:

- Calderdale Council;
- Royal Berkshire NHS Foundation Trust;
- Siemens Global Business Services;
- Wärtsilä Marine Power.

Special thanks to Professor Leslie Willcocks for writing the foreword and patiently reviewing the interim versions of the book. I would like to say a big thank you to Pascal Bornet, Dr Adam Bujak, Robert Hughes and Professor Mary Lacity for reviewing the advanced draft of the book and for the feedback that they provided.

As part of the research for this book, I interviewed a number of AI-in-business experts, users, practitioners, analysts and advisers. I am indebted to them for sharing their perspectives and views of how the market is going and evolving. My thanks to:

- Adam Bujak, CEO and Co-Founder, KYP.ai;
- Akeel Attar, CEO and Co-Founder, XpertRule;
- Alex Bentley, Chief Revenue Officer, XpertRule;

- Bill Thomas, Co-Founder and Chairman, Emergence Partners;
- Darrien Bold, National Digital Lead for Stroke, NHS England and NHS Improvement;
- David Poole, CEO and Co-Founder, Emergence Partners;
- Eric Simonson, Managing Partner, Everest Group;
- Fred Laluyaux, CEO, Aera Technology;
- Dr George Harston, Chief Medical and Innovation Officer, Brainomix;
- Gerry Brown, CX Research Director, IDC Europe;
- Dr Hannah Dee, Senior Lecturer in Computer Science, Aberystwyth University, a computer vision specialist and co-author of *Women in Tech*;
- Harri Lemmelä, Development Manager, Customer Applications, Wärtsilä Marine Power;
- John O'Connell, Director of Strategic and Service Innovation and Transformation Director, Data Analytics and Artificial Intelligence, NHS South, Central and West;
- Dr K. Nagaratnam, Consultant Stroke Physician and Geriatrician Clinical Lead for Stroke Medicine, Clinical Lead (Acute), Royal Berkshire NHSFT and ISDN Buckinghamshire, Oxfordshire and Berkshire;
- Laetitia Cailleteau, DATA + AI Europe Lead, Conversational AI Global Lead, Accenture;
- Martha Bennett, Vice President and Principal Analyst, Forrester;
- Dr Michalis Papadakis, CEO and Co-Founder, Brainomix;
- Nikolas Barth, Head of Digital Transformation and Strategy, Global Business Services, Siemens AG;
- Pascal Bornet, author of *Intelligent Automation*;
- Riaz Rahman, VP Healthcare Global, Brainomix;
- Richard Boyd, Principal Consultant, XpertRule;
- Robert Hughes, Co-Founder and CEO, Techopian;
- Toni Kershaw, Customer Access Manager, Calderdale Council.

ABBREVIATIONS

AI	artificial intelligence
API	application programming interface
BFSI	banking, financial services and insurance
BoM	bill of materials
BPM	business process management
CapEx	capital expense
CPG	consumer packaged goods
CPQ	configure price quote
CRM	customer relationship management
CT/CTA	computerised tomography angiography
ERP	enterprise resource planning
EU	European Union
FTE	full-time equivalent
HR	human resources
IA	intelligent automation
IDP	intelligent document processing
IoT	Internet of Things
IPA	intelligent process automation, often referred to as intelligent automation
IT	information technology
IVA	intelligent virtual agent/assistant
IVT	intravenous thrombolysis
JRH	John Radcliffe Hospital
KYC	know your customer
LVO	large vessel occlusion
ML	machine learning
MT	mechanical thrombectomy
NLG	natural language generation
NLP	natural language processing
NLU	natural language understanding
NPC	non-player character

OCR	optical character recognition
ONS	Office for National Statistics
OpEx	operating expense
P2P	Purchase to Pay
PO	purchase order
PoC	proof of concept
RBFT	Royal Berkshire NHS Foundation Trust
RDA	robotic desktop automation
ReLU	Rectified Linear Unit
REST APIs	RESTful application programming interfaces
RoI	return on investment
RPA	robotic process automation
SLA	service level agreement
SSC	shared services concept
SSV	skill-shortage vacancy
TITAN	Thrombectomy Innovation and Transformation Network
UI	user interface

GLOSSARY

Anterior circulation: The blood supply to the front of the brain.

Application programming interface (API): An API allows software to connect to other software. It is a documented and standardised interface through which programs can connect and provide services to each other.

Artificial intelligence (AI): Refers to systems designed by humans that, given a complex goal, act in the physical or digital world by perceiving their environment, to build intelligent entities (Lowe and Lawless, 2020).

Attended automation: This is a term used in the field of robotic process automation to refer to robots that are activated by humans and that return controls to humans after completing their tasks (as opposed to being run according to predefined schedules or set off by events).

Banking, financial services and insurance (BFSI): The name for the financial services industry that includes banks and insurance companies.

Bill of materials (BoM): The complete list of materials and components used in making a product.

Business process management (BPM): The science of managing business processes and the software solutions that support it.

Capital expense (CapEx): Expenditure on capital items such as equipment, software and real estate.

Computer vision: The technology and techniques that allow machines to capture information from pictures, images, three-dimensional objects, scans, videos and other visual inputs.

Computerised tomography angiography (CT/CTA): A type of scanning of the human body that uses contrasting material injected into the blood to identify health problems with blood vessels and related diseases.

Configure price quote (CPQ): A category of software that allows sales teams to configure a product according to the customer's requirements and preferences, to allow them to estimate the price of the product to produce a quote.

Constraint inference: Understanding the consequences of constraints on automated decision-making.

Decision tree: A decision-support tool that models decisions and their consequences in the context of a specific business requirement, setting or scenario.

Desktop mining: A field of process mining that gathers data from human interactions on a computer, for example mouse and keyboard clicks and screen image capture.

Enterprise resource planning (ERP): A group of software solutions to manage and run business processes including finances, supply chain and human resources.

Full-time equivalent (FTE): A unit used as a measure of the workload of a full-time employee.

Image recognition: A subset of computer vision, which classifies images.

Intelligent automation (IA): A term that describes a spectrum of software solutions that are used to automate business processes. These typically include a mix of intelligent and non-intelligent software such as chatbots and robotic process automation (RPA).

Intelligent document processing (IDP): A category of software that uses natural language processing (NLP) and other intelligent capabilities to automate processes that handle documents.

Intelligent process automation (IPA): Using intelligent automation software to automate business processes.

Intelligent virtual agent/assistant (IVA): Software that can process language, speech and text to offer services that would otherwise be provided by contact centre agents, or act as a virtual assistant to people.

Internet of Things (IoT): The network created as a result of devices and hardware being connected to the internet, therefore allowing humans and other devices to monitor them and communicate with them.

Intravenous thrombolysis (IVT): Delivery of drugs intravenously to eliminate blood clots that can form in the brains of stroke patients.

Ischaemic change: Changes to small blood vessels, in the context of this book, caused by lack of blood and oxygen after a stroke.

Know your customer (KYC): A regulatory requirement in financial services to authenticate the identity of customers as part of offering them services.

Large vessel occlusion (LVO): Large blood clot.

Line of business (LOB): Refers to processes through which a business earns its revenue.

Mechanical thrombectomy (MT): A procedure to remove large blood clots from the brains of stroke patients.

Natural language generation (NLG): The techniques applied in software to generate words and sentences and interact with humans through natural languages by processing unstructured data.

Natural language processing (NLP): Techniques used in computing to process language. It has two primary components: natural language understanding (NLU) and natural language generation (NLG), described below and above, respectively.

Natural language understanding (NLU): Techniques used to enable machines to understand natural language. A part of natural language processing (NLP), described above.

Neural network (NN): An artificial network of neurons or nodes used for predictive modelling in artificial intelligence.

Optical character recognition (OCR): Technology that enables text in scanned images to be converted to machine-readable characters, and thus allowing documents to be processed electronically.

Phygital: Refers to the field of technology that aims to bring the digital and physical worlds together by offering services that flow from one into the other.

Posterior circulation: The blood supply to the back of the brain.

Process discovery: A field of software that helps organisations find information about their processes. A part of process mining described below. In more recent years it is often used to refer to tools that identify manual processes that can be automated using intelligent automation software.

Process mining: Refers to the use of software that mines data held in program logs to build a virtual view of how processes are run in the organisation, to capture information about them to allow organisations to improve and optimise the processes and to provide reports with process insights.

Purchase order (PO): Used in enterprise procurement to manage orders and invoices.

Purchase to Pay (P2P): The end-to-end process of procuring and receiving goods and services, and paying and accounting for them in business.

Rectified Linear Unit (ReLU): An activation function in neural networks.

RESTful application programming interfaces (REST APIs): These are connecting interfaces between computer programs that adhere to representational state transfer (REST) architecture, collectively referred to as RESTful APIs.

Return on investment (RoI): The quantitative benefits that you realise from investing in assets such as hardware and software, as a proportion of the cost of purchasing them, and having them built, installed and run.

Robotic desktop automation (RDA): A class of software solutions that are activated by a user to automate a process on their desktop and then return control to the user. It is a term that is often used interchangeably with 'attended automation'.

Robotic process automation (RPA): A class of software that automates processes by connecting to business systems through the user interface, and thus mimicking the way humans work, for example logging in to a system and entering new data into a field, filling in a form and pressing submit.

Service level agreement (SLA): The agreed level of service to be delivered by a team, business unit or external service provider/contractor.

Text analytics: The process of deriving information from text sources in computing.

Unattended automation: Automation that is activated by systems to run according to predefined schedules, timetables or events.

User interface (UI): This is the layer of software that is used for interacting with users, typically via a physical or soft keyboard, mouse, touchpad, touchscreen, joystick, pen, and voice and gesture commands.

USEFUL WEBSITES

https://www.turing.ac.uk/
The Alan Turing Institute.

https://www.aboutamazon.com/news/amazon-ai
Amazon AI.

https://machinelearning.apple.com/
Apple machine learning research.

www.bcs-sgai.org/
The BCS SGAI, the specialist interest group on AI.

https://ai.google/
Google AI.

https://www.ibm.com/cloud/learn/what-is-artificial-intelligence
IBM AI.

https://www.imperial.ac.uk/computing/research/artificial-intelligence/
Imperial College AI.

https://keras.io/
Keras.

https://www.microsoft.com/en-gb/ai/experience-ai
Microsoft AI.

https://news.mit.edu/topic/artificial-intelligence2
MIT AI news.

https://openai.com/
Open AI.

https://www.research.ox.ac.uk/area/ai
Oxford University research on AI.

https://www.tensorflow.org/
TensorFlow.

https://www.cam.ac.uk/topics/Artificial-intelligence
University of Cambridge AI.

PREFACE

I wrote this book simply because I had a lot to say about artificial intelligence (AI), its role in business process automation and the road that organisations are taking towards becoming autonomous enterprises. I believe it is important to consider where this development is taking us and understand the nature of the change that is already happening, the opportunities that we are gaining and the risks we are facing. It is by seeing the bigger picture that we can make decisions, whether to take small, measured risks or embrace change in a 'Big Bang' approach and become more innovative and efficient in what we do.

While I have a lot to say, I do not wish to blind readers with the science of AI. Accordingly, I have provided only a high-level introduction to it and to intelligent automation technologies, but I hope enough to make sense of the content of the book and to convey the messages that are needed to managers and decision-makers to help organisations surf the tide of change.

Importantly, I want to emphasise the fact that you can take advantage of AI to speed your journey of change without needing to become an expert in the science of it, because computer scientists and big and small technology vendors are already doing the work for you.

AI has applications in many different fields and it would be impossible to cover it all in one book. I have focused mine on the work that people do in corporate offices, which is commonly known as knowledge work, and is undertaken as part of their daily business processes. I have focused on knowledge work because it is changing fast and its automation will be the bedrock of autonomous enterprises of the future.

I apologise in advance for the use of a lot of IT industry and corporate jargon. Should you need it, there is a list of abbreviations complemented with a glossary of terms in the front of this book.

It has been a pleasure to write this book, part of which entailed conducting a host of interviews with experienced practitioners on how they deployed AI in their organisations. I connected to many knowledgeable and thoughtful industry experts and pundits to share our perspectives. I can honestly say that the research has enriched my knowledge and has made me hungrier for more. If I can impart a fraction of this enthusiasm to you by sharing my thoughts in this book, then I will have succeeded.

PART 1:
THE RISE OF THE AUTONOMOUS ENTERPRISE

The autonomous enterprise has been in the making for centuries with every human-led technological development and advancement contributing to it. In this part of the book I describe the concept of the autonomous enterprise and the role that artificial intelligence (AI) plays in its creation. Firstly, I explain the whys and wherefores of using AI in business. These include the drivers for and the patterns of its adoption by enterprises. I provide an overview of the most dominant technological approaches to AI and its potential for innovation and efficiency. Importantly, I define the key concept of the autonomous enterprise powered by AI, and cover the technologies that are making it possible.

1   INTRODUCTION AND OVERVIEW

The ever increasing automation of knowledge work combined with transactional process automation are leading to what I call the **autonomous enterprise**. I introduce this concept and explain how artificial intelligence (AI) is making it a reality in this chapter.

I explore how AI powers innovation that in turn leads to new models of business that are largely automated. I examine the business imperative that is efficiency and how this is driving business process automation and how that in turn is leading organisations along the road to autonomy. Furthermore, I look at the patterns of adoption of AI and how organisations are falling behind the curve.

WHAT IS THE AUTONOMOUS ENTERPRISE AND WHY DO WE NEED TO LEARN ABOUT IT?

A few decades ago it was impossible to imagine that car manufacturing processes would be almost entirely automated, with people supervising robots and control systems. Yet, this is exactly how things are done today and have been for a while too. Over the years, this high level of automation of manufacturing processes from manual to mechanised and robotised has been emulated and adopted by other industries, for example logistics and warehousing, travel and agriculture. Today it is starting to happen in an altogether different part of businesses and that is autonomous knowledge work, the kind of work that requires know-how and both objective and subjective decision-making.

Two major forces are driving enterprises towards more autonomy: efficiency and innovation. Pressures of a competitive market keep organisations searching for more output per unit cost and many AI-powered solutions support this objective. Similarly AI is powering the drive for innovation as large and small companies disrupt the market by bringing out novel products and services. The rush for innovation is fuelled by money pouring into the sector from investors and governments.

These two realities are coming together and leading to rapid technical advances. However, it is clear that adoption of AI is being led by large technology platform companies and start-ups. Yet, there is still plenty of potential for organisations of any type, as I explain later in this chapter and throughout the book, to tap AI to innovate and become more competitive.

This increasing level of automation of knowledge work combined with other transactional process automation is leading to what I call the autonomous enterprise, which I define in this chapter and explore extensively in Chapter 9.

In this book I focus on automation of knowledge work, but we are moving beyond the rush to digitalise these types of processes, combining them with automation in the physical world. This combination of physical and digital is being increasingly referred to as 'phygital'. I address some aspects of phygital in this book as well.

Knowledge work varies from basic transactional data entry and skills-based manipulation of the data, to capturing information via interactions with others by reading documents, emails, texts and messages, looking at images or talking to people on the phone and chatting on the web. Through these interactions, knowledge workers capture information, make some form of assessment and do the necessary work or advise others based on the information, their skills and decisions. Automation of this kind of work using software with AI is in its early phases of development and adoption. Today, it is typically applied to simpler processes where the decisions to be made are not very complex, for example does the purchase order (PO) in this invoice match our records and is the amount correct? The main difference from past office work automation is the evolving ability of machines to read and digest unstructured data, that is information that you typically get in documents, including images and pictures, and from voice, speech and sounds.

This is in contrast to our ability to automate processes that use structured data – data that are already put into structures in a database that non-intelligent software can work with easily. Processes using structured data form the bulk of business transactions – something that we have been able to automate one way or another for decades using computer software such as spreadsheets, helping us with complex calculations and data analysis, or customer relationship management (CRM) software that helps us manage customer information, contact details, past interactions, purchase histories and so on.

Today, we are able to automate processes that handle unstructured data thanks to intelligent software. These solutions can capture information from the unstructured data and use them to make simple decisions, for example whether to approve an invoice for payment and to activate the payment process.

The more basic and earlier approaches to automating processes that use unstructured data have involved optical character recognition (OCR). The more basic IDP tool, after scanning, digitises the content of paper-based documents and allows some level of automated processing of the content. Documents that can be processed with more basic capabilities are usually highly structured in templates that the software can handle. With advances in technology we can automate a lot more today, with machines able to recognise important pieces of information in unstructured documents as well as the context and the sentiment based on the use of words in the document. Methods of capturing the information have also moved well beyond OCR, from barcodes to QR codes, image and shape recognition and voice processing. The ability of machines to interact with the physical world and capture unstructured data from it has come a long way. Today, there are advanced solutions that can not only understand speech in the business context but also ordinary human utterances, as well as detecting sentiment in the tone of voice during telephone calls.

It is not just advancements in the way that we can take unstructured data into our computer systems that is allowing us to take advantage of AI, but the development of many technology ecosystems that support it. An overview of some of the most prominent ecosystems and toolkits that have made AI accessible and available for use by organisations is provided in Chapter 2.

When you combine knowledge work automation with that of other office processes, for example the kind of transactional data processing that enterprise software systems have enabled us to do for years, such as using accounting or procurement software, then companies can automate processes of low complexity from end to end. Over time with more advances in AI-enabled software we will be able to automate progressively more complex knowledge-based processes, and many of them end to end. By doing so we will achieve a significant step change in efficiency, for example not only replying to a customer on a chat channel online but assessing the tone of the conversation and determining if there is a risk of customer attrition, then making a decision about offering them a discount on the price of a product, all automatically.

Automation increases efficiency with higher levels of straight through processing, faster response times, reduced data errors, elimination of duplicated effort, and making up for any shortages of staff and skills. These in turn lead to business outcomes such as lowered costs and higher profitability, increased capacity to take on more work to grow the business, and higher levels of customer satisfaction and brand loyalty. Existing examples include companies reporting more than a 60 per cent reduction in the cost of running some processes, adding capacity of between 100 and 500 full-time equivalent (FTE) employees, and 100 per cent reduction in process errors (Everest Group, 2020) thanks to their adoption of intelligent solutions.

With increased automation of knowledge work, enterprises can also capture more data systematically from their enterprise software, and be able to use AI to analyse the data quickly for deep business insights. AI can be used to join the dots to reveal hidden patterns that spell issues such as operational bottlenecks, fraudulent claims, poor performance, lack of regulatory compliance, supply chain problems and more. One example is that of Ocado, the UK online grocer, that conducts millions of demand forecasts a day using machine learning algorithms (Blake, 2021) to ensure quantity and freshness of its stock to minimise food waste. It also takes advantage of AI and data science to maintain a digital twin – a virtual model of the operations – to simulate its operations (Slegers, 2021) to be able to optimise its processes end to end. In its 2019 annual report (Ocado Group, 2019) it stated that, thanks to further technological improvements to its end-to-end operational capabilities across demand forecasting, inventory management and fulfilment, it had halved its food supply waste from 0.8 per cent to just 0.4 per cent of its sales. This is a double saving of costs, and food that did not end up in the waste bin.

Similar AI-powered analysis and forecasting can help organisations to spot opportunities for optimising processes, and improving or designing new products and services, therefore boosting their ability to innovate and gain a competitive edge. With innovation they can be the ones that disrupt the market rather than be disrupted by others.

AI in the form of analytics, and with its ability to spot patterns, can help enterprises even before their processes are automated. For example, one breed of software called intelligent process mining is already at work in some enterprises, identifying problems such as hundreds of variations in processes that are supposed to be highly standardised. Lack of standardisation spells complexity and cost. Minimising variations in how processes are done by different people and parts of the organisation directly benefits the business bottom line. In some cases process mining software is finding huge deviations from best practice and regulatory compliance as well. In these cases, the intelligent software is identifying not only where processes could be improved but helping the organisations to minimise risks, for example of incurring hefty regulatory fines and damage to their reputation.

THE BIRTH OF THE AUTONOMOUS ENTERPRISE

With intelligent technology enabling us to boost efficiency and innovation and minimising risks, the case for AI in business grows and consequently, over time, we will see increased adoption. More and more of the high-volume repetitive transactions that make up the core functions of the enterprise will be automated, just like manufacturing processes did several decades ago. This will give rise to the autonomous enterprise. This is an enterprise that:

- Conducts its core daily business functions in a digital and automated manner with minimum human touchpoints, with AI embedded in many of its systems.

- Employs people that do fewer repetitive tasks, such as checking and settling invoices, and more complex and strategic work, such as handling sensitive and complicated customer cases.

- Automates not only major operations, but empowers staff to automate their own repetitive tasks as well. The autonomous enterprise provides intelligent automation (IA) and augmentation technologies to its staff to help them work more efficiently and productively. It also offers training and support to ensure that they can use those technologies effectively.

- Takes advantage of operational data to create digital twins – virtual models of some of its critical processes – to make sure that work flows through the organisation efficiently and that there are data available to support both automated and human decision-making.

- Analyses data not only to make better operational decisions, but to provide support for strategic decisions, and to manage the business and risks better and to innovate.

The transactional work that machines do within an autonomous enterprise includes data entry, checking huge numbers of documents for information, cross referencing and checking data for accuracy, answering simple and repetitive enquiries at any helpdesk or in customer interactions.

The higher value work that people do in an autonomous enterprise includes designing, implementing, overseeing and improving the automated business processes, handling cases or enquiries that are too complex for the AI to complete, planning and implementing routines for the AI to capture business intelligence from daily automated operations, and then from the analysis of the business intelligence, finding opportunities for improving services and products and to increase revenue. Accordingly, they will design new products and services, plan business growth and geographic expansion and so on.

Organisations that have successfully integrated their data across multiple systems can go further by feeding their advanced analytics solutions, sometimes referred to as cognitive systems, with the data. This will allow the solutions to come up with answers to questions fast to guide decision-making on the fly and even have AI recommend actions, identify more opportunities for automation or activate automated procedures based on live operational indicators.

The tools that empower the employees in the autonomous enterprise include digital personal assistants that take dictation and, in more advanced cases, arrange meetings and book conference rooms or calls on behalf of the worker. Software will provide them with collaboration, best answers based on historical information – answers provided in the past to similar questions by their colleagues – and signposting to documents that show how similar requirements have been dealt with by the organisation before and more.

Examples of employee tools that are already available include predictive text in email, voice-activated commands on personal productivity software, briefings from virtual assistants on personal computers that on a daily basis remind us of commitments and follow-ups to be done and prompt us to book focus time in our diaries. This is not automation but assistance and augmentation of human work, helping people to become more productive and better at what they do.

There are already very successful examples of autonomous enterprises in existence today. Many online retailers such as Amazon and Ocado have highly automated their core functions such as sales, order fulfilment and stock controls.

Ocado conducts its business through a web-based shopfront powered by an online catalogue of products. Much of its order processing and customer interactions are digitalised. It is the same story in the order fulfilment function, which is automated with Ocado robots picking items from stocks and packing the customers' orders to be dispatched. Although many of its daily business operations are automated, there are many people at work at the company too. Behind the scenes, humans are busy building new capabilities for the company, creating new features for its website, and carrying out supply chain and order fulfilment functions. They are building partnerships and choosing and buying technology to enhance operations and more.

As a result of its digital and automated approach to selling groceries, Ocado has been able to grow and capture a strong share of the crowded UK online grocery market, estimated at 14 per cent according to Ocado's 2020 annual report (Ocado Group, 2020). It has been able to develop its technology and take advantage of it in multiple deals, as part of which it provides online grocery services for other major supermarkets. It is also expanding beyond the shores of the UK and building an international presence.

As another example, there is a new breed of financial services company that challenges large and established players through the use of innovative intelligent technologies.

These challenger banks and insurance companies run highly automated operations using AI that speed up customer onboarding as well as other business processes, for example know your customer (KYC) identity checks for account openings, loan approvals, administration and servicing, or fully automated insurance quote, claims assessment and settlement processes.

Many people are afraid of this level of automation and in particular of the threat of job losses. That is understandable; after all, with technology to automate the work that humans have always done, what will be left for humans to do? Are humans destined to a life of unemployment misery? This is unlikely. Automation of daily business functions should not spell the end of work for humans but a change in the way that we conduct work and the nature of it. Gone will be jobs involving very repetitive and high-volume tasks such as data entry. Instead humans will be required to design, implement, manage, oversee and maintain automated processes and manage the technologies that power them. There will also be more creative roles, for example designers of customer journeys through the autonomous enterprise, to ensure the quality of service and great customer experiences. As for the employees of the organisations, the autonomous enterprise will enable them not only to do more interesting work but to do it better and faster.

There are other factors too that will mean humans will continue to have work, for example the existing shortage of skills in many industries, and aging populations in a lot of countries with low birth rates. Consequently, change is already on its way, firstly, with more technology-oriented jobs across all sectors. Secondly, demand for people in other sectors increasing, for example the creative, hospitality and care sectors, and consequently making up for some of the losses in other sectors due to automation. For example, Eurostat, the statistical office of the European Union (EU), reports that accommodation and food services followed by arts, entertainment and recreation, and administrative and support services accounted for the highest share of recent job starters in the EU (Eurostat, 2021). When combined, they accounted for nearly a quarter of all job starters at 23 per cent. Eurostat describes 'recent job starters' as recently employed, having started their job in the three months prior to the survey interview. The findings may well be simply the bounce back from lockdowns during the pandemic but there are other trends at work too. In the hospitality and entertainment sectors, for example, demand is increasing for more variety of experiences, including virtual reality and services offered digitally to people at home, for food and beverage deliveries, as well as increased hygiene requirements and safeguarding in venues. I believe these are all contributing to the trend reported by Eurostat. More on this topic follows in Chapter 10.

In the rest of the book, I focus mainly on two things that AI in business enables, and these are increased opportunities for innovation and efficiency through automation.

In recent decades, technology-powered innovation has led to a wave of companies that disrupt whole industries with new products and services or revolutionary operating models that rapidly gain market share and leave established players behind. Examples include Tesla, Netflix, Uber and Airbnb. The success of these companies has led to a flood of ambitious entrepreneurs wanting to emulate their success by setting up their own technology start-ups. There is a growing industry too of investors whose business is to spot the next tech-led disrupter to invest in. Subsequently, money has been pouring into AI start-ups. According to research by CSET, part of Georgetown University (Arnold, Rahkovsky and Huang, 2020), in 2019, $40 billion was invested in AI companies by a mix of organisations from venture capital and private equity firms through to enterprises that engaged in mergers and acquisitions. These are disclosed investments that numbered 3,100 in separate transactions. There would have been many more that were not disclosed.

Governments are getting in on the act too as they strive to make their countries the next leading technology nation in the world. Across the globe, governments are implementing ambitious plans to fund technology, and in particular AI powered start-ups, to generate wealth and jobs for their citizens. For example, the EU White Paper On Artificial Intelligence – A European approach to excellence and trust, published in 2020 (European Union, 2020), sets out its ambitions to attract more than €20 billion of investment in AI each year for the next decade. The paper also highlights that in the previous three years, EU funding for research and innovation for AI rose by 70 per cent to €1.5 billion but that it lagged investments in AI in North America at €12.1 billion and in Asia at €6.5 billion.

In May 2019 the UK Government announced its AI sector deal to harness AI and big data as one of the great opportunities of our age (UK Government, 2019). The deal is to provide a package of nearly £1 billion of support for the sector, with contributions from the Government, industry and academia, with £603 million in newly allocated funding and up to £342 million from existing budgets, alongside £250 million for connected and autonomous vehicles.

With investment pouring into the sector, more innovation and disruption is certain to happen and no organisation can afford to be left behind. This is why I cover innovation both in this chapter and in more detail in Chapter 3.

Business efficiency has been a priority for every boardroom since time began with enterprises taking all kinds of measures to achieve it. I will recap some of these measures and how AI can change them later in this chapter and in more detail in Chapter 4.

AI FOR INNOVATION

I came across a good example of innovative uses of AI a couple of years ago when I visited a healthcare company in San Francisco. Although a start-up, its healthcare app had already been adopted by various business customers around the world. The healthcare app ran on mobile phones and remotely connected doctors to patients for health advice and consultation via video calls. This was innovative at the time but it wasn't the only feature of the technology-enabled service. The app also used AI to check the patients' symptoms and to connect them to doctors with a track record of dealing with similar conditions or illnesses. The AI conversed with the patient and used their health records to determine the probable cause of the problem before referring them to a doctor. Additionally, it pooled advice that had been provided previously by doctors for similar conditions to provide information to the patient. The app had already been adopted by a healthcare insurance firm to provide improved and differentiated services to its clients and the start-up had more prospects on the horizon.

On another occasion, I visited a large German manufacturer to see its use of AI in manufacturing process simulation, visualisation and digital twins (in this case a digital version of the human worker at their workstation). These provided information on how to optimise the manufacturing processes as well as the ergonomics of the human workstation on assembly lines. The more its processes were optimised the faster it could manufacture its products as well as keep its staff happy and comfortable during their shifts.

Another time, in an innovation centre in Silicon Valley, I saw a futuristic demonstration of AI in eLearning in 3D using holographic imagery that would guide field engineers to fix broken machinery at customer sites. This type of solution has good potential for field operations, including maintenance of vending machines and repair of home appliances.

More recently, I learnt about a new feature that an IA vendor has added to its solution to partially automate the coding of robots in its robotic process automation (RPA) software, using process mining and AI. This speeds up process automation and consequently the return on investment (RoI) in the technology. Firstly, the task of identifying candidate processes for automating with RPA is accelerated using the process mining component of the software. Secondly, the codification of the identified process is made faster using the semi-automated intelligent robot code generation. This is a very exciting development for me because a few years ago I predicted that RPA software would enable the automation of automations – robots generating the software code for new robots (Burnett, 2019). The technologists among you will be familiar with low- and no-code development environments. This solution takes the concept further by first discovering what process could be automated and then the automatic automation of that process.

These are very different examples of uses of AI but, in all the cases, the companies have grabbed the opportunity offered by AI to develop innovative solutions. The history of business is strewn with examples of innovations that have disrupted industries and transformed one or more aspects of work or social models, for example cloud computing, social media and companies that have disrupted whole industries such as Uber and Airbnb. For every company that advances thanks to its innovation, there are many that fail to change.

Enterprises cannot afford to fall behind in AI-powered innovation because there are market forces that are driving it and billions of pounds of private equity and other money pouring into the sector, as discussed previously.

AI is a particularly good enabler of innovation because firstly, it allows us to automate things that we couldn't have done before, for example reading unstructured documents and humans conversing with machines in natural languages. Secondly, it brings us insights through advanced analytics, fast.

I was involved in an AI learning project recently. The exercise was to write code to test the likelihood of a banking customer registering for a new service. The analysis took into account various factors such as the customer's income and past history. We used Python and a neural network provided by Keras (Keras, n.d.), an open library that works on top of TensorFlow (TensorFlow Learn, n.d.), using a large anonymised dataset. In this very basic learning exercise, we were able to get accuracy of prediction of over 92 per cent. The whole thing took us one-and-a-half days, spread over a number of days, and that included debugging the code. This type of operational analytics would have required new ways of thinking if we were using more traditional statistical analysis tools. The actual analysis, the algorithm running through the data, would have taken a long time as well without a neural network. The potential of this type of rapid operational analysis is huge and I encourage you to think of the possibilities for your organisation.

Keras is just one of many libraries that are available to the world to learn and practice AI for real. Chapter 2 provides an introduction to some of these types of resources as well as the science of AI.

AI FOR EFFICIENCY

In the context of this book, efficiency is the effectiveness with which a company conducts its business. It is the amount of work that it does and the costs that it incurs compared with the results that it achieves. It is a simple maths equation and if the balance tilts too much towards expenses and work and energy expended, then costs accumulate and profits decline. If this type of scenario continues and no action is taken to address it, a downward spiral begins that could result in the company going out of business.

Efficiency is something that organisations have strived for since the dawn of commerce. Here is a quick recap of the measures most frequently used in the late 20th and 21st centuries:

- Methodologies such as Lean, Six Sigma and Agile: Lean and Six Sigma were extremely popular approaches for process and business optimisation for decades. More recently Agile has been adopted for business management but its roots are steeped in best practice for software projects. Software solutions for business process management and optimisation are increasingly being used as well.

- Centralisation and shared services concepts (SSCs) and practice: shared services took the concept of specialist bureaus that emerged in the 1950s further to deliver dedicated, expert, standardised and quality services to a group of business units within large companies, for example finance and accounting services, human resources (HR) or customer contact services. In this model, the parent companies transfer the need for business function and process efficiency to the centre managers. Often, they make them responsible for their centre's commercial viability and increasing year-on-year efficiency. The managers, in turn, invest in skills, systems and process standardisation to ensure continuous improvement to meet their performance targets. That said, after years of year-on-year improvements, many SSC managers say that they run out of options to achieve yet more demanding efficiency targets set by their parent companies. This is why they welcome developments in technology that allow them to do more for less.

- Labour arbitrage, off-shoring and near-shoring: the location of shared services became an important aspect of cost efficiency as well with shared services centres being placed in countries where the cost of staffing them was lower than western Europe or North America. Later, the model evolved further with more specialist services being placed closer to home, for example in Eastern Europe for Western European businesses, or South America for North American companies. Today, companies use a mix of off-shore, near-shore and on-shore (in the home country) shared services centres to optimise the model according to the specialisation of each centre. For example, you might have general accounting and transactional finance services off-shore, the management of the finance software near-shore and strategic management on-shore. The labour arbitrage equation is getting diluted with salaries going up because of a shortage of skills in many popular off-shore and near-shore delivery locations. Another challenge in off-shore locations, is the relatively high price of software licences when currency exchange rates are taken into account. The cost can become a barrier to investment.

- Outsourcing: this is another step in the continued search for business efficiency. In outsourcing, a whole function or a group of business services are outsourced to specialist outsourcing companies, who deliver them either as a specific or as part of a shared services model from off-, near- or on-shore locations, either using their own software platforms, for example banking systems for banking clients, or the client's own systems, which they access remotely. Outsourcing companies continually invest in technology, methodologies and skills in order to offer specialist services at attractive prices. They also offer different models of services such as dedicated and pooled, with options and different pricing levels that include contributing to the modernisation of a service, gainshare and outcome-based pricing. More automation in their clients' enterprises, however, will no doubt impact their business models.

- Digitalisation of services: investing in new systems, typically cloud-native solutions that run on cloud infrastructure, has been a key pillar of transforming and modernising the corporate technology landscape. This reduces the upfront costs of investment and turns capital expense (CapEx) into operational expense (OpEx) that can be absorbed by the business throughout the year. Digitalisation also supports the pivot to online services with virtual self-service becoming the standard way of interacting with customers. Self-service is an incredibly efficient way of providing customers with information about products and services as well as allowing them to choose and customise what they want and order it all from the comfort of their computers. The model provides fast and complete virtualisation of services with, ideally, the only customer contact being at the point of delivery.

Of course, digitalisation can result in reduced social and business contact for people and cause problems for those who do not have access to technology. Many businesses continue to offer alternative channels of interactions, for example banks offering phone and branch-based banking, but governments need to act to ensure that those channels do not disappear completely over time.

Each lever mentioned above is capable of generating efficiency savings to some degree and when combined together, as is often practised by businesses, significant benefits can be achieved. Add AI-enabled capabilities and the outcomes can be considerably boosted. The term 'a step change' is used too often in the context of business process efficiency but there is evidence to show that it is true when AI is involved. In 2020 Everest Group (Everest Group, 2020) assessed 49 enterprises for the maturity of their adoption of IA solutions.

> IA is a term that refers to adoption of a combination of non-intelligent solutions such as RPA, and intelligent solutions with AI embedded in them, such as intelligent document processing (IDP) and chatbots, to automate processes.

The Everest Group report, based on its research, identified eight of the companies that it assessed as Pinnacle enterprises. These had outperformed the rest of the group in terms of the sophistication and maturity of their adoption of IA and the results that they had achieved. The research found that: 50 per cent of the Pinnacle enterprises had achieved cost savings of more than 60 per cent with IA in the process area that the technology had been applied; the other 50 per cent reported savings of between 20 per cent and 60 per cent in the same context. Also, out of the remaining group of 41 companies, only 29 per cent had achieved cost savings of over 60 per cent, and 44 per cent had achieved cost savings of between 20 per cent and 60 per cent.

The results are highlighted in Figure 1.1.

Figure 1.1 Impact of IA initiatives on costs – percentage of respondents (Source: Everest Group, 2020)

13

AI was one of the major factors that separated the eight top performers, the Pinnacle enterprises, from the rest of the group of companies:

- A total of 75% of the Pinnacle enterprises had deployed machine learning for document classification and data extraction.

- A total of 63% had also deployed intelligent capabilities for computers to process documents and natural language, known as Natural Language Processing (NLP) and text analytics.

- The remaining 41 enterprises showed far lower adoption of AI, with only 38% having adopted machine learning for document classification and data extraction.

- Only 22% of the rest had adopted more advanced NLP and text analytics.

These results are shown in the chart in Figure 1.2.

Figure 1.2 Sophistication level of OCR/IDP deployed – percentage of respondents
(Source: Everest Group, 2020)

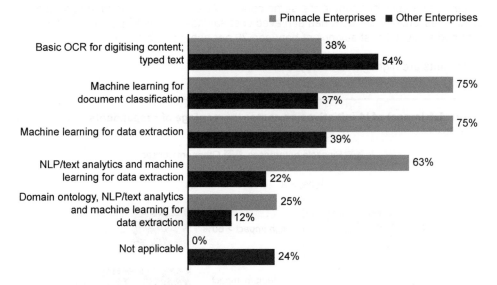

While not the whole of the phenomenal savings achieved by the Pinnacle enterprises in the Everest Group report can be attributed to AI alone, it is clear that AI can substantially lift efficiency. The other significant contributing factors to the outcomes were the application of some of the measures that I have already covered; firstly, optimising processes before automating them and secondly, sharing resources. The Pinnacle enterprises had bet heavily on best practice and this too had paid off for them. They harnessed the power of AI and machine-learning technology and combined it with the rigor of their approach.

Other studies have shown that AI can deliver significant benefits. In one programme called FUDIPO (FUDIPO, 2016), AI was shown to reduce energy consumption when used for plant-wide monitoring and control of data-intensive processes. FUDIPO comprised a set of proofs of concepts (PoCs) conducted as part of a European Commission-funded project under the H2020 programme, SPIRE-02-2016 topic and in partnership with Mälardalen University in Sweden. It ran between 2016 and 2020. The PoCs found that the use of AI for predictive data analysis and controls resulted in energy savings in various industries including oil refineries and water treatment plants. The findings show that the application of AI in the context of monitoring and control of data-intensive processes can generate huge energy savings when applied in different industries. The preliminary results were published by Open Access Government (Open Access Government, 2020; Dahlquist, 2020) showing the following levels of energy savings were possible per year based on the FUDIPO PoCs:

- 86–95 terawatt hours per year (TWh/y) in pulp and paper processing;
- 120–200 TWh/y in oil refineries;
- 17–41 TWh/y in wastewater treatment.

These would add up to total savings of 353–526 TWh/y, equivalent to three per cent of all energy used within the EU for all purposes.

When AI is combined with other technologies it amplifies efficiency by enabling more of each business process to be automated than is possible when using non-intelligent software alone. This is primarily because it allows companies to automate processes that handle both transactional data that is structured data, and unstructured data in documents and other types of content. It can also take data from sources such as files or devices, and analyse them to provide predictive analytics and intelligent controls. Consequently, more of each process can be automated, with straight through processing increased substantially. AI can also enhance or replace the other efficiency levers that I have described above, as shown in Table 1.1.

Table 1.1 How AI can enhance the more traditional levers that companies have used for business efficiency

Traditional lever	Examples of how AI can boost the outcomes
Methodologies such as Lean, Six Sigma and Agile	Process mining software, powered by AI, can identify process optimisation opportunities at a detailed level and provide comprehensive operational and performance intelligence to allow companies to improve business functions and productivity levels.
Centralisation and SSCs and practice	With the potential of other more traditional levers for efficiency exhausted, SSCs are increasingly looking at intelligent solutions to achieve additional year-on-year efficiency savings. This includes use of technology to digitalise and automate processes, e.g. by increasing the use of chatbots and virtual assistants to handle incoming enquiries, and adding AI-enabled next-best-action advice to improve productivity and response times in to contact centres, information technology (IT), HR or other helpdesk functions.

(Continued)

Table 1.1 (Continued)

Traditional lever	Examples of how AI can boost the outcomes
Labour arbitrage, off-shoring and near-shoring	Partial automation can boost employee productivity no matter where they are located. It can free up office workers to do more interesting work as well, e.g. from doing basic data entry to being retrained to work in an automation centre of excellence or do other more complex work such as production of management reports. IA can also change the location needs of the organisation, and increase the use of near-shore or on-shore resources while keeping costs low. This is not good news for the mass production and outsourcing service centres of the world, but they too are building their AI skills to improve the efficiency of their services to continue to offer attractive propositions to other countries. Additionally, they are expanding more and more into software and technology product development.
Outsourcing	Increasing levels of automation in outsourcing contracts can lead to adoption of different pricing models, changing from input/headcount-based pricing to outcome or gainshare models. More services could be brought in-house while those that remain outsourced could deliver additional benefits such as service providers being able to increase year-on-year efficiency savings thanks to the insights that they get when they automate their processes.
Digitalisation of services	Digital transformation has been going on for years but it is evolving. With AI, digital can become intelligent; that is, software-based business and consumer solutions that use AI in some form or other, e.g. the healthcare app that uses AI to check the user's symptoms. The number of solutions that take advantage of AI in some form or other is increasing fast. The uses are not limited to end-user applications but also to how companies find insights and information, how they optimise and automate their business processes, transport and logistics operations and more. AI can be used to better maintain IT infrastructure and systems and improve desktop support. Another use case is automatically managing and monitoring devices and machinery thanks to AI checking their status via the Internet of Things (IoT) and analysing the data that it gathers. Even traditional businesses such as farming and agriculture are starting to adopt AI, be it in the form of intelligent weeding of crops to robots picking fruit and vegetables, or autonomous farm vehicles.

GOING FROM DIGITAL TO PHYGITAL

Levels of automation and augmentation of operations and processes in enterprises have been increasing steadily over the two past decades. Until recently, all the attention was on increasing virtual interactions and digitalisation of processes enabling customer self-service and personalisation. The COVID-19 pandemic with its lockdowns and the shift to working from home increased the take-up of digital channels, while behind the scenes, organisations invested in automation of processes to make up for staff shortages due to the pandemic. As the digitalisation of processes continues, we will increasingly need to join the digital world to the physical world. It is the combination of the two that is referred to as phygital (physical+digital). Examples include taking orders for products online and then having automated order fulfilment processes, such as robots in the warehouse, to get the physical product to the client. These are the kinds of extensively automated processes that we will see more of in the autonomous enterprises of the future. I provide many examples of phygital throughout the book and in particular in Chapter 3, where I examine the opportunities for innovation with AI.

To illustrate the concept in this chapter I focus on its application in marketing.

The marketing automation imperative in a phygital world

In the context of marketing, one challenge for enterprises that have made digital their main channel of interactions with their customers is to do better than their competitors and differentiate their online capabilities, shopfronts and apps from others. The result is a host of offerings that often bridge the divide between the physical and digital worlds. For example:

- Retailers that provide apps for improved in-store shopping experiences, for example customise and order online, then try and buy in store with your order identified using the store app on your mobile phone.
- Offers on single tariffs for electricity at home and for electric cars combined with a smart and connected electricity meter in the home.
- Phone companies that offer tickets for entertainment and experiences that are highly in demand.

Managing such arrays of offerings requires a lot of administration and handling of data that would need to be updated across multiple systems with confirmations, notifications, alerts and information sent to the customer, as well as partners, service providers, company divisions and operational teams. These create a huge workload for every organisation that offers them. In the autonomous enterprise, these transactions would be mostly automated in a joined-up fashion.

The capture of transactional data to be analysed for insights, such as the customer's buying patterns and preferences, is not a new thing, but in the autonomous enterprise these would be powered by AI to gain better personalised services, offers and more business intelligence such as propensity to buy a new product or likelihood of applying for a new store card.

The same automated approach can be used to help with managing customer contact better, for example if changes to the customer's data are automatically propagated across systems, it ensures that they are always up to date. Consequently, should a client call the customer contact number, in the autonomous enterprise both robots and human agents will have access to the latest customer information to handle the call quickly and efficiently.

AI ADOPTION

Research that I conducted for this book between November 2020 and January 2021 shows that many organisations are still at the beginning of AI adoption. The purpose of this research was to find out which companies were advertising for AI skills in the UK. The study examined 200 unique non-academic AI-related job vacancies advertised on two major job sites. It found that 60 per cent of the 200 were posted by technology companies, start-ups or consultancies that needed skills either to build or enhance their own AI-powered products or have skills in place for client projects. The split of job adverts by enterprises on the sell side of the market, that is technology vendors, consultancies and service providers, versus the buy side of the market, for instance buyers of technologies and related services, is shown in Figure 1.3.

Figure 1.3 The split of adverts for AI skills by sell side and buy side of the technology market

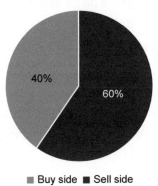

■ Buy side ■ Sell side

Advertisers from companies that were not in the business of selling technology-based solutions or related services were in the minority, accounting for 40 per cent of the adverts. These included banks, insurance and telecommunication companies, car manufacturers, and a small number of primary healthcare providers. Many of these companies were major global businesses, some with their own technology arms, that you would expect to see on the list.

In terms of industries, the computer software and technology-related services industry significantly dominated the jobs market, and in second place but considerably behind was banking, financial services and insurance (BFSI). AI skills were in high demand in the healthcare industry too, unsurprising given that the study was conducted during the COVID-19 pandemic at the end of 2020. The 200 vacancies were advertised by 116 unique named organisations and 41 unknowns that were advertising through agencies.

The study showed that there is a lot of AI-based development going on in the market. There were adverts by major global technology platform companies but also many private equity-funded start-ups developing solutions for specific industries, from healthcare, financial risk and sports analytics to solutions for fashion and retail, better performance in computer games and better software development environments including automation of coding.

Figure 1.4 shows the split of job adverts for AI skills by industry from November 2020 to January 2021.

Figure 1.4 Job adverts for AI skills by industry

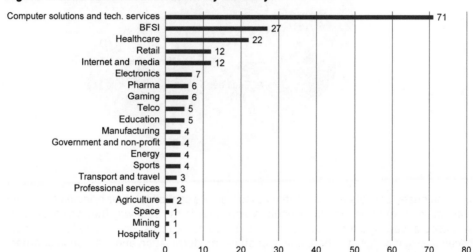

In terms of roles advertised, most in demand were data scientists, and AI and machine learning (ML) engineers. Figure 1.5 shows the frequency of adverts by job type. In this context, it is important to note that there was much overlap between job descriptions. For example, adverts for ML or AI researchers often mentioned the need for the candidate to work on data science projects, and engineers needed for data science and vice versa.

During the same period, jobs advertised for skills in specific packaged AI business solutions, such as IDP software, were few and far between. Furthermore, ads by consultancies and professional services firms for those packaged solutions outnumbered those by end-user enterprises by two to one.

This state of a new technology market is not unusual when software vendors and professional services companies are the first to adopt that new technology. The point is that AI can bring big benefits to businesses and there is an ever present risk of disruption. These are driving adoption of AI by big business, but others cannot afford to stand still.

Unsurprisingly, the giants of the technology industry were well represented in the sample. While we cannot necessarily emulate what these massive companies can do

Figure 1.5 Jobs by role type

with their deep pockets and unlimited resources, we can follow their principles of never standing still, and investing in technology and skills in the best way that we can, to gain and keep a leading edge in our own lines of business. Investing in AI today is a must because, like it or not, it is here and is enabling modernisation and disruption of orders of a magnitude bigger than any previous technology.

I cover what AI is in Chapter 2 but only to set the scene without going too deep into the science of it. My reason for this is that computer scientists are developing intelligent solutions and AI platforms for us. Businesses only need to understand the basics and to learn the art of the possible with a host of free and commercial AI resources and products out there in the software market.

SUMMARY

In this chapter I have provided a round-up of all the most important topics related to AI in business, including its ability to automate operations and, importantly, knowledge work; the journey that we are on towards the autonomous enterprise; the increased focus on phygital; the power of AI to help enterprises innovate and make a step change in efficiency; the future of work for humans and the current state of AI adoption by enterprises.

In the rest of the book I delve deeper into these topics, starting with an overview of the science of AI in the next chapter.

2   WHAT YOU NEED TO KNOW ABOUT AI

Anyone's imagination would be stretched by the possibilities presented by AI today. Its current capabilities and rate of development provide the potential for new types of enterprise and service.

As you think about the innovation or efficiency initiatives that might move your organisation towards an autonomous enterprise, you need to know a few facts about AI:

- It is a disruptive technology and so you can expect your own market to change. At the end of the chapter I suggest how you can start now and lead that disruption rather than wait for others to take the initiative.

- One impact of AI is that enterprises will look at IT with a different perspective. This has happened before when many organisations found they had to reorganise to make use of the web and mobile technologies. AI will extend this need for change and in this book I explain some of the new roles required to make the most of the more intelligent components.

- Solutions will rapidly evolve to meet common requirements. In this book, I use the loose term 'toolkits' to describe this range of solutions. They range from packaged software with the ability to configure some AI features, through to technically complex code libraries and everything in between. It is a new market so the catch-all term 'toolkit' covers all the different types of software that have emerged.

- You will probably need to build relationships with new vendors or reassess how much development you take on in-house as your AI initiatives progress. In this chapter I describe some signs of things to come and predict the types of products and vendors that will spring up.

Before going into detail about these practical considerations I provide a bit of historical background and then talk about the types of solutions that are being developed in the market. I then describe some of the underlying technology. Some readers may want to skip the more technical sections or go back to them for reference. I then circle back to the types of solution that are available, or soon will be, and from there provide some guidance on the key decisions to be taken as you look at your organisation afresh.

THE EVOLUTION OF AI AND WHY IT IS RAPIDLY ADVANCING NOW

AI has a long history, first in the minds of theoretical mathematicians and computer scientists, then in sci-fi movies and from there into the real world. From the 1950s to the 1980s progress was relatively slow. Computers could be programmed to perform specific tasks at incredible speed. To a limited degree these programs could 'learn' and improve. Milestones such as Deep Blue's chess victory over Gary Kasparov in 1997 grabbed headlines. It then took another two decades before AlphaGo beat a professional player, Fan Hui (Williams, 2019), an event that underscored the advance into the more abstract reasoning required by the game of Go. AI was still not making a big impact on our business or domestic lives but in the last three or four years the technology has permeated into our everyday routines and the pace of this is quickening.

To distil the aspects of this technology that will be useful to a business manager, I explain the new market for tools that allow AI to be applied directly to a business problem. For most enterprises and government organisations the best way to use AI is through a software tool that allows a business problem to be addressed directly. In this book, I call software products of that type a toolkit. These toolkits allow a business function to be configured in a non-technical environment by a team who understand the business problem to be addressed but who do not want to get involved in technical implementation detail. There are many toolkits and they provide functions as varied as automated document processing and hazard avoidance through to eRecruitment and conversational interfaces on enterprise resource planning (ERP) systems.

This chapter describes the types of toolkit available and then goes into some detail about the machine learning and, in particular, the deep learning technology on which many of them rely. Having delved into the underpinning technology, I go back to the types of toolkits to explain how they can best be used and the skills needed to exploit them.

BREAKING IT DOWN: MAKING AI WORK FOR YOU

The technical environment you need in order to get the benefits from AI will be influenced by many factors specific to your own organisation's history, resources and future direction. On the assumption that few will be able to establish a business case to create AI solutions from scratch, most will use one or several of the many toolkits available. The market for toolkits is relatively new and is changing fast. To put some structure on this rapidly evolving landscape, I first classify the toolkits into the type of problem they are addressing.

Figure 2.1 illustrates this classification and below I describe the layers in more detail.

The top of the diagram represents the layer that interacts with people or maybe other machines, across all the different types of toolkits: a speech interface, a conversational text-based interface or any other type of interaction.

The rest of the layers, the toolkits currently in the market that provide AI, can then be split into four major categories:

- Configurable business solutions that use AI as an embedded element.
- Business function toolkits that can present a user interface directly or are intended to be used by a higher level business solution.

- Specific functions that can be assembled together, for example document processing requires NLP as well as aspects of image recognition.
- Underlying technology toolkits that provide facilities for building and training deep learning systems but without needing to get down to the detail.

Figure 2.1 Overview of the types of AI toolkit

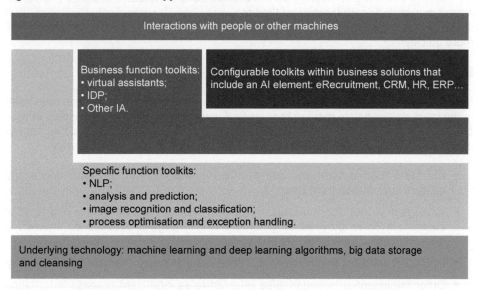

I am going to take a look at each layer in Figure 2.1 and the types of toolkit in turn to help you select the group that meets your business need or area of interest.

Configurable toolkits within business solutions

Every major vendor of packaged applications for the enterprise market has made announcements about their current and future use of AI. If your organisation has existing investments in these applications, then exploring their AI roadmap would be a good starting point. Most include:

- conversational user interfaces;
- more automated processes, particularly interfaces with customers and suppliers;
- better predictions from analytics modules;
- automated advice for employees: for example next best action for call centre agents;
- automated advice for customers: such as conversational diagnostic guides and virtual customer service agents;
- devices that are automatically monitored, possibly in combination with the IoT.

The aim of each vendor is to make their solutions comprehensive enough for their market while also keeping the solutions easy to use and easy to configure. The list is illustrative and is being expanded all the time as vendors build or acquire new functionality. The advantage of following a vendor roadmap is that the development and integration risks are handled by the supplier but it is unlikely to be the least costly approach and will always lag the state-of-the-art by a few release cycles. The lag is caused by the time required by the vendor to implement new features and complete the required compatibility testing across a broad suite of modules and also provide an acceptable upgrade path for the installed software base. Unsurprisingly, this means that single product vendors and open-source projects can usually release new functionality more quickly.

Business function toolkits

It may be that packaged applications do not allow your business to differentiate itself in the marketplace or are moving too slowly. If you determine that some aspect of your business has specific needs, then there are toolkits for many purposes and the range is expanding daily. Those on the market typically cover one of the following areas:

- IDP systems that scan and interpret forms, reports and correspondence and capture information from them.

- Intelligent virtual agents/assistants (IVAs) that can provide a service to your customers or employees by guiding them through processes or answering questions about your products and services.

- Intelligent analytics that try to predict, for example, a customer's propensity to buy.

- Other intelligent automation, also referred to as intelligent process automation (IPA) that allows organisations to start to move away from processes that are defined once and get re-engineered periodically to business flows that can continually improve.

At the time of writing there are toolkits that allow you to uncover processes within your organisation (process or task mining), spot patterns in customer behaviour to help develop products, or detect fraud and processing mistakes.

I think the market will settle on some specific AI functions that are used across many organisations and a new form of packaged software market will emerge. Software in this new market will draw less of a distinction between defining a function or process at 'design time' and then continuing with that process in production until it is re-engineered. Rather the software itself will guide the analyst and developer towards a solution that satisfies the business requirement, taking into account the results from real data along the way. The solution will not be static but will continue to learn.

Learning is an inherent aspect of AI but in Chapter 3 of this book we explore the impact on a typical software development cycle. There are signs that tooling will emerge that applies AI to the design of processes as well as the execution of those processes. I believe this could make a fundamental difference to the way organisations view their software development projects, but will leave further discussion to Chapter 3.

Specific function toolkits

Continuing our journey down the layers of toolkits illustrated in Figure 2.1, it may be that you evaluate the business function toolkits that are available and decide that none of them meets your business needs, in which case there are products that allow you to more directly manage the AI. From the research that I have conducted for this book, and the case studies in it and other sources, it is clear that most of the current applications of AI in business today rest on one of the following four specific functions:

- NLP using both text and speech;
- data analysis, classification and prediction;
- image recognition and classification;
- process optimisation and exception handling.

There are many other problems that can be addressed by AI but most of the examples in this book use toolkits that include one or more of these capabilities. Looking at the same situation from an alternative viewpoint, most toolkits that are available as a product are covered by this list.

Natural language processing

NLP is the technology that allows speech and text to be analysed and used within software systems. It is the technology used by the virtual assistant on your phone that responds to your voice commands. Language processing is now so good that many more uses are opening up. You can use NLP directly in your projects by, for example, running all your customer comments for a week through a sentiment analysis tool to understand whether your service or product is improving. If you get that same feedback in the form of documents from, say, intermediaries in the supply chain, then the combination of NLP and image recognition have greatly improved the reliability of automated document handling and consequently made the analysis of feedback more comprehensive and reliable.

NLP underpins all the conversational interfaces and speech recognition technology used in the examples in this chapter. If you want to ease your organisation into AI then NLP could be a good place to start.

Data analysis and prediction

The same family of technologies that have advanced language processing can be applied to many prediction tasks. What is the likelihood of default on a credit card account? What healthcare outcome can we expect from a set of personal or population data?

As long as you have sufficient good quality data to train the AI, then you can use them to look for patterns in the behaviour of your products, customers and partners. You can then predict the likelihood of key events, for example customers switching or purchasing something, or partners defecting.

Image recognition and object detection

Image recognition is used for mainstream applications such as number plate recognition, and there are countless other applications of image and object recognition that confer significant business advantage, such as:

- recognising a spare part from a photo sent in by a customer;
- diagnosing a fault from a photograph of an appliance combined with an error code from the same image;
- damage assessment during insurance claim processing;
- enhancing business processes and models if the image or object recognition is sufficiently reliable.

Huge improvements in image classification systems were highlighted by the renowned ImageNet Large Scale Visual Recognition Challenge. From 2010 to 2017 the performance of the contender systems continually improved and overtook the ability of humans in this space. Specific milestones came with the use of convolutional neural networks (Image-net.org, 2014; Markoff, 2014). With developments in this field, the commercially available toolkits get close to the performance seen in these competitions and can be delivered using commodity cloud infrastructures, therefore many processes that rely on images can be reassessed. For example, an organisation that repairs or replaces car windscreens could use image processing to remotely assess the viability of repairing a chip in the glass as opposed to replacing the whole screen before visiting the customer to fix the chip, therefore being able to better optimise supplies and schedule time for the repair.

It is important that the technology is deployed with due regard for its social impact. Face recognition, for example, has to be handled particularly carefully and the recent withdrawal of some large software companies from such recognition projects has highlighted the ethical concerns that need to be addressed before solutions are deployed. These very important social considerations are handled separately in this book in Chapter 10.

Process optimisation and exception handling
The business processes that are the lifeblood of organisations have been examined, re-engineered and changed as different management methodologies find favour, as described in Chapters 1 and 3. AI can be used to provide a new perspective.

Many automated processes are plagued by exceptions that require human intervention, for example when, due to duplicated records in a database, the identity and residential address of a person cannot be confirmed automatically, or when a chatbot cannot handle a conversation because it is beyond its training. Exceptions like these are passed to humans to handle. The people involved with these processes soon get to understand the reason for the failure of the automated process when faced with the exceptions, but can make process changes to iron out the exceptions, depending on their priorities and the availability of resources to make the changes.

AI is very good at finding patterns in unstructured data and these can be used to automate exception handling. For example, you have been running the same process in accounts payable for two years. You are finding that 10 per cent of invoices need some manual intervention before they can be receipted. You either re-engineer the processes or you can automatically classify the exception and then automate the corrective action. You can call in some consultants or you can run the historic data through a neural network and find out what led to the exceptions. Neural networks are very good at finding a way to make predictions from data but not so good at explaining why those predictions work. This is a research field that is advancing rapidly. Why were invoice mistakes more common on a Friday? What led to the discount period being missed most frequently? These exceptions can be discovered by people but a neural network will look for patterns that are not prejudiced by experience. If there is a pattern, a neural network will find it and your domain experts can determine the root cause. If there is no pattern in the data, you will find that too and save a bunch on fees.

You may be thinking of applications that are way beyond the mainstream examples described so far. If you are, you may need to look beneath the hood to see if the underlying neural network technology can be used directly to bring your idea to life.

Key underlying technologies

The toolkits that provide specific business functions are built on underlying AI capability. This section describes how that underlying technology works and provides some pointers to more detailed material. You do not need to understand the technology to use the various toolkits on the market but it will be useful if you need to communicate with vendors or technical teams.

Each of the functional areas I have covered in the previous section rely on three key technologies: machine learning, deep learning and big data.

- **Machine learning** – The general ability of a machine to learn from data and adapt its behaviour. In the context of this book, software systems that can predict or classify using training data and then apply that learning to real data. Neural networks are an important class of machine learning systems and are the focus of this chapter.

- **Deep learning** – An extension to machine learning in the form of multi-layer neural networks that can learn more sophisticated ways of interpreting the training data to predict an outcome. Although this appears to be a minor extension to machine learning, the combination of many additional network layers, large amounts of training data and improvements in the technology used within the network layers led to a major advance in the performance of these deep learning systems in the early 2010s, and consequently brought about the advances in intelligent technology that we see today.

- **Big data** – For a deep learning system to work properly it needs to be trained using a representative amount of data. In many applications that means a very large set of data. Along with the advances in AI, the ability to store and manage very large datasets has been a key parallel technology and development. Very simple AI produces good results when fed with very large amounts of good data. The best AI will produce poor results if there is not enough data or those data are of poor quality.

These three types of technologies are used in conjunction with neural networks so a brief explanation of how these software structures work is needed to understand why we are in the middle of such a revolution.

Neural networks

When logic no longer fuelled AI development the parallel study of neural networks took over. This field drew inspiration from biology and the structure of the brain to build machines that 'learnt' how to predict or classify without being given any information about the structure of the problem to be solved, just a large amount of training data with the expected result. Once the machine learned to produce output that was close enough to the expected result, then it could classify or predict using actual data, as long as the training data were sufficiently representative.

A simple neural network will take a number of inputs and feed them through layers of artificial cells loosely modelled on biological neurons. Each cell takes a weighted input from the previous layer that is then aggregated with the other inputs to form an output that is fed to the following layer. The inputs are usually arrays of floating point numbers and the weight is a scaling factor which represents the importance of that input to the performance of the overall network. The larger the weight, the more the output of the cell is influenced by the input. In Figure 2.2 an input layer is connected to a single hidden layer and then that in turn is connected to an output layer with a single node. Although production systems have more layers and complexity, this is the essence of a neural network.

Figure 2.2 A simple neural network

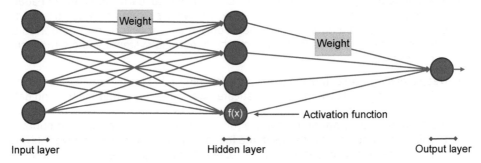

For a neural network to produce useful outputs it has to be trained by running representative data through the network and then adapting the weights on each connection between cells to achieve the best result.

Multi-layered neural networks
To find the secret to the success of neural networks and their use in deep learning, we must delve a bit further into how they work (see Figure 2.3).

Networks for deep learning are characterised by multiple layers. Anything above four layers is deemed to be in the realms of deep learning.

The first layer handles the input from the data (training, test and real data). The intermediate layers, or hidden layers, process the results of the previous layer and finally feed an output layer which provides the result that the designer is looking for, for example categorisation of an image, prediction of a result, or classification of a spoken phrase.

Figure 2.3 A multi-layered neural network

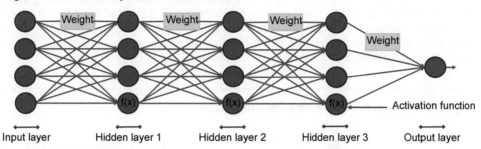

Deep learning produces such accurate results because of the interaction of the multiple layers and the training algorithms that adjust the weights. In the next sections I describe how this happens.

The role of hidden layers

The power of deep learning comes with the implementation of hidden layers. The hidden layers provide flexibility so that the whole model adapts itself to the task in hand. As long as the basic design of the network is suitable for the type of problem in hand and the training data are sufficient then the training algorithms will do the rest. The type of decisions that data scientists and engineers have to make are:

- number of layers;
- the connectedness of each layer;
- the aggregation functions (called activation functions) to use in each layer.

The number of layers   There is no consensus on a foolproof way of deciding the number of layers in a neural network for any single problem type. It may seem odd but some level of trial-and-error is needed. Many classification and prediction problems just require one or two hidden layers. It is probably best to start simple and add layers if the prediction results are not adequate.

Connectedness   How connected does the network have to be? You can start by saying that every cell needs to be connected to every cell in the next layer (a dense network) but this configuration uses considerable resources. Neural networks use a lot of computing power so after the first few experiments it may be beneficial to move to a sparser network.

Activation functions   For each layer, there is a choice of mathematical function that is applied to all the inputs to compute the output. The selected function is called an activation function. In practice a small number of functions are commonly used and a surprising fact is that one of those functions, called 'ReLu' (Deep AI, n.d.), produced a step change in the ability of neural networks to find optimal solutions for real-world problems. Some researchers (Feng and Shengnan, 2019) put the recent success of deep learning down to widespread adoption of this seemingly simple function.

Training the network

Neural networks learn by adjusting the weights while running through training data. The weights are adjusted to improve the performance of the network by reducing the difference between the output of the network and the training data. This difference is called the loss and you can imagine the function relating the loss to the weights as a surface, as illustrated in Figure 2.4.

Figure 2.4 Neural networks try to minimise loss

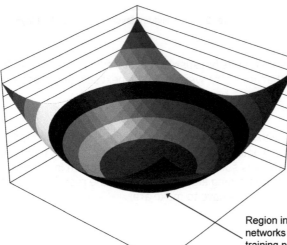

The loss function represents the difference between the prediction and the actual outcome. The neural network is trained so that the weights in all the layers are adjusted to minimise the loss function. The loss function can be represented as a bowl with each weight being one of the three dimensions.

Region in which the loss is minimised so neural networks try to adjust their weights through the training process to produce a loss as close to the bottom of the bowl as possible.

The surface will have a region where the loss takes on a minimum value, so it can be thought of as a bowl shape. In reality the surface would be uneven with many ripples and features but it does not affect the overall objective, which is to find the set of weights that minimise the loss. Put another way, we need to find our way to the bottom of the bowl from any starting point on the surface, so this is the objective of the learning process.

Loss functions and their role in guiding the learning process   After each iteration, or batch of iterations, through the training data the loss function is evaluated. This function tells the machine the magnitude of the difference between its predictions and the actual results recorded in the training data. The same loss function can be used to say in which direction the weights need to be adjusted, but it does not say how much by, so that decision is left to the designer of the network (see Figure 2.5).

The practicalities of sourcing training data   It is no coincidence that good results are coming from applications that can supply large amounts of data. All the large cloud platform providers have access to data on a global scale. They also get good results from their NLP, analytics, search and image classification.

In a commercial setting, as part of considering whether an AI solution can produce good results, the availability of training data and the quality of the ongoing actual data should be considered very carefully. There are many types of problems for which you do not need to provide the data because you can get toolkits that have already been trained.

Figure 2.5 Adjusting weights to minimise loss

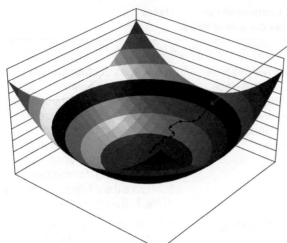

Step 1. The slope of the bowl surface is computed at the point represented by the initial weights.

Step 2. Weights are then adjusted slightly in the direction of the bottom of the bowl.

Step 3. The loss function is then recalculated. The overall value of the loss function should have reduced and by repeating iterations of steps 1 to 3 the loss function will track towards the bottom of the bowl.

If you need to source your own training data then you need to make sure they are available in enough volume. Many successful AI solutions use millions of records. These data then have to be of good enough quality, and a representative sample of the information that they are representing, in order for them to be a valid training set. If a measurement technique for one of the attributes changed halfway through the sample then the data would need some attention before they could be used for training and this all requires expertise.

Neural networks are not difficult in concept but in practice the large amounts of data involved and the technical implementations needed to allow them to perform adequately mean there are many components and design decisions needed before a system can work in production. Luckily, the world recognised that to make this type of AI solution workable, toolkits were needed so that the people with the business problem were not faced with many detailed implementation questions.

Having delved into some of the workings of neural networks, the following sections come back up a level and describe how the technology is being packaged for business use into different types of toolkit.

Making the most out of toolkits

Vendors and organisations have surrounded the underlying technologies with toolkits that make them usable in enterprises without them having to reinvent the wheel. The huge investment in the AI market means that vendor and open-source offerings have developed to the point where there are many credible options for enterprises of all scales. In practical terms, many decisions about the use of AI technology will hinge on the vendor/toolkit/framework you wish to adopt. So here I will break down the level of tooling that is available and, depending on the type of organisation you work for, the choices that you might choose to make. You will not need to delve into the neural networks themselves; the dashboards and configuration editors will be all you need to get the business outcome you require.

Table 2.1 summarises types of toolkit, the functionality available, the team/skills mix that you might need and examples of how the toolkits can be used.

Table 2.1 The toolkits and the functionality available, with user examples

Type of toolkit	Examples	Functionality or use case examples	Users
Configurable business solutions			
Finance systems	Intelligent forecasting or fraud prevention, radically different conversational user interfaces	Conversational user interface, intelligence analytics, and guidance on next-steps	Many types of office workers, e.g. staff in the finance department, financial business analysts and staff engaged in managing inventories in manufacturing or fraud prevention in insurance, business analysts who can configure the intelligent features of the software for the users
HR	Recruitment solutions	CV screening	HR/recruitment analysts, business analysts who can configure the intelligent features of the software for the users
Customer relations management	Customer journey and contact management, solutions for customer service agents	IVAs added to CRM solutions can provide conversational interfaces for customers, or intelligent assistants for customer service agents	Customer contact managers have these implemented by technical specialists for use by their customers and contact centre agents. Customer journey analysts can analyse the data from these interactions to design better customer journeys. A good example of this is provided in Chapter 6, the Calderdale Council case study. Business analysts can configure the intelligent features of the software for the users including agents
Toolkits for business functions			
IDP	Form interpretation and uploading, e.g. mortgage application forms Unstructured document tagging and filing	Parse and interpret text, field identification and interpretation Categorisation of unstructured text, tagging text with an industry specific lexicon	Toolkit configuration experts use these solutions to create products for end users such as those handling invoices, and bank account and loan application forms, or handling service support enquiries. A good example of this is provided in Chapter 5, in the Siemens Global Business Services case study where support tickets are processed automatically

(Continued)

Table 2.1 (Continued)

Type of toolkit	Examples	Functionality or use case examples	Users
Virtual agents	Customer query handling	Automated responses to questions, dialogue design tools	From personal assistants on our mobile phones and devices to chatbots on websites, these can be deployed by technology and toolkit experts to provide digital services through conversational interfaces to customers, and provide data for insights and analysis to customer journey analysts, tone-of-voice experts
	Conversational user interface for forms	Conversation designer to navigate a customer through complex forms	
	Avatars or virtual character as seen in some games	While still limited to use in gaming, in future we might see the use of avatars to represent people, who are working remotely, at meetings	
	Mobile phone personal assistants	Facilities to allow you to integrate your offerings into existing phone personal assistants, for example adding a voice interface to your app	
	Virtual call centre agents	Dialogue design studios, integration with telephony systems, configurable NLP	
Intelligent analytics	Targeted marketing	Used in marketing and advertising to target specific groups of potential buyers, understand their propensity to buy a new product or service or predict risks of customers defecting to competitors or defaulting on payments	Data analysts and data scientists analyse the data and produce reports for marketeers, or provide instant analytics online to make special offers or make recommendations, e.g. 'people who bought this also bought that'. Sales and finance teams use these to increase revenue and prevent losses
	Buying habits analysis and predictions		
	Risk analysis		

(Continued)

Table 2.1 (Continued)

Type of toolkit	Examples	Functionality or use case examples	Users
IA/IPA	Process mining	Used to find process pathways in the organisation and any bottlenecks or deviations from standard operating models. It can also be used to identify opportunities for further automation	Set up by tool configuration specialists and used by operational team leaders, process analysts, and data analysts to optimise processes
	Intelligent exception handling[1]	A virtual agent learning from humans how to handle unusual cases	
Toolkits for specific technical functions			
NLP	Libraries are available for most popular platforms. An open-source example is NLTK (Natural Language Toolkit, n.d.) that runs on Python	All the popular libraries include parsing and tagging to attach a domain or project specific meaning to language segments	Data scientists with the necessary programming skills for your chosen platform
Analysis and prediction	An example is Facebook's Prophet, an open-source tool for forecasting (Facebook Prophet, n.d.)	Configurable models, with interpretable and adjustable parameters that analysts can use to make forecasts and predictions	Data scientists with the necessary programming skills for your chosen platform

(Continued)

1 Exceptions are cases that automations cannot handle due to complexity or ambiguity of the information associated with them or simply that are too sensitive to be handled by machines, for example cases of bereavement.

Table 2.1 (Continued)

Type of toolkit	Examples	Functionality or use case examples	Users
Image recognition and classification	Many open-source image processing libraries. Commercial utilities and web-hosted versions from the large platform companies	From a stream of images or video the tools can classify the content and recognise objects. The configuration facilities provided by the tools vary. Some are code libraries, others have configuration studios	Depending on the tool, you will probably need programmers and AI analysts if only to integrate the results of the classification or recognition into the rest of your business process. Once integrated, business users or software robots in automated processes can take advantage of it for cross-referencing information or object recognition, e.g. identifying weeds in fields of food crops, taking stock on supermarket shelves, counting items in a delivery pack or checking identity, e.g. as used by governments in passport and driver licence applications
Process optimisation and exception handling	AI reconciliation platforms, automated break processing in financial services, process mining and IA/IPA tools	Functionality is changing rapidly in this relatively new category. Tools help to define the new optimised processes based on existing usage and data. Exceptions are increasingly automated	Business analysts will be needed with both process and technical skills, the nature of which will be largely specific to the toolset selected. When this type of software is configured, it can be used by team leaders, subject matter experts, people in charge of process efficiency and optimisation

More general frameworks

So you have reviewed what your application vendors can supply and looked at toolkits tied to a particular functional area but the business transformation you have planned needs more. The next step is to consider one of the frameworks that are supplied by the large platform vendors, the big open-source projects and the new challengers.

If you want your AI investment to build a lasting differentiation against your competitors or to disrupt a market then this is probably where you want to be. In this section I provide pointers for you to follow with some comments. The market is moving so fast that no printed list will be current for long so here I shamelessly point to web resources.

I love generalised frameworks. To make use of them you will need a team of data scientists. This is a much more specialist skill set than the business analyst who might configure the toolkits above. Maybe you have a team of data scientists already in place but if not, then it will be the people, not the technology, that dominate your spend if you adopt a generalised framework to build your own competitive advantage.

All the major platform players offer frameworks that can be used to create and manage neural networks including:

- Tensorflow (TensorFlow Learn, n.d.) from Google.
- Microsoft's Azure Cognitive Services (Microsoft Azure, n.d.).
- Pytorch (Pytorch, n.d.) sponsored by Facebook.
- Amazon Web Services (AWS) and its adoption of the Apache mxnet technology with SageMaker (Amazon, n.d.).
- Apple's CoreML (Apple, n.d. (b)) in conjunction with its on-device Apple Neural Engine (ANE) (Apple, n.d. (a)).

Each of these frameworks is different in nature and those differences will steer your choices. If you start going down this route you will need to evaluate each of these and more against your project objectives. The choice of framework is important because once you have invested in a framework you will not want to change quickly.

These are not sector specific toolkits but if you are in a highly regulated industry, you will have to ensure that the technologies that you select adhere to the relevant regulations, for example the required security and standards for transparency and human supervision of automated decision-making. The offerings from the technology giants listed above will almost certainly have the accreditations needed for such requirements but it is worth checking.

Path to success

With such dramatic results being achieved by the best AI projects the rewards are high. Needless to say, there are significant risks as well. Here are my lessons on the path to success with AI, learnt from my research, the case studies in this book and other customer engagements:

1. Some of the technology is new and quite complex so keep your implementation as simple as it can be while proving that your objective can be realised.

2. Either use simple AI with a very large amount of data (e.g. likelihood of customer defection)

3. or use a toolkit to encapsulate the complexity and use a team who are close to the business sponsors to configure high-value quick wins. Simple virtual agents to take the load off call centre staff and IDP to automate the handling of forms with unstructured text are both good examples.

4. If you need to differentiate your business by custom-building your own neural networks then recognise that payroll costs will dominate your investment because you will need a team to build and continuously evolve the solution.

These general paths to success then require management action to support them.

Management considerations

Apart from the technical aspects to these transformation projects, there are important management actions that business and organisation leaders should consider to support their innovation initiatives:

1. Strategies to manage disruption in your own market.

2. Organisational changes to address the challenges of AI.

3. Changes to IT and vendor strategies.

I will cover each of these in the following sections.

Market disruption
Managing a business through disruptive times is difficult. It almost certainly means placing some bets beyond the traditional comfort zone of the decision-makers. Those aspects of your business that most differentiate you in your marketplace are probably a good place to start, with some experiments that will probably involve limited investment but significant commitment from internal and external personnel, such as your subject matter experts and consultants with AI implementation skills.

Based on the case studies in this book, and the advice from successful adopters of AI, start several radical projects and fail early. Those that succeed could be your growth drivers through this wave of change.

Organisational change
Once you get a feel for the type of change your business needs to make, then consider the implications for your organisation. New ways of thinking and new interfaces with stakeholders need the correct organisational structure to support them. New roles will include data scientists who look at internal and external information and can work with others in your organisation to see new possibilities. Human interface designers will be able to project the right tone and image through dialogues and avatars.

It is very important to assess your organisation's current state and ask:

- Does your organisation want to move out of its comfort zone and embrace new business models?

- Can you challenge the current state and think of radical new futures for your organisation?

- Does your organisation have the skills to investigate new solutions, particularly in data science?

- Can you recast the human interface with customers, employees and other stakeholders?

Others have found that having decided on an approach, organisational changes are needed to empower the new roles of AI analysts and data scientists. AI analysts ensure that the end-to-end interaction between the AI implementation and the stakeholders achieves the planned objectives. Data scientists forge the links between the available information and the learning systems. Depending on the scope of your deployments, these roles might represent individuals or large teams but they are relatively new skill sets and will require the organisational structure to change if they are to be empowered to make the necessary changes in IT and operational departments.

IT and vendor strategy

AI and its associated technologies have changed the IT market. Further changes will follow as the many hundreds of toolkits jostle for dominance. You will probably need to forge relationships with a few of the toolkit vendors to support sufficient innovation in your projects as you blaze a trail for your organisation. At the same time your traditional vendors can probably offer safer alternative, if slower, paths and so they too need to be brought on board with your thinking.

SUMMARY

In this chapter I provided a brief overview of the science behind the, currently, most dominant approach to AI using neural networks. To provide context, I provided some of the history of the main developments, some of which are really quite technical. The good news is that, for most of us, that technical detail can be accessed using 'toolkits' which provide the functionality we need without exposing us to the inner workings of AI. These toolkits are themselves rapidly evolving so I put forward a classification that should help select those that you want to work with.

For readers who want to understand a bit more about neural networks, I went on to explain how these structures work. Some remarkable results can be obtained with relatively simple neural networks. Nonetheless, it is the incorporation of this technology into the context of every enterprise that holds the promise of rapid advances. At the end of the chapter I discussed some of the matters that managers should consider about the broader organisational implications of AI. This sets the scene for the next chapter in which I look at the impact of AI on innovation.

3   AI FOR INNOVATION

In this chapter I explore how AI is proving to be a catalyst for innovation in a business environment.

First I ask why AI is so important in innovation. I then go on to look at how it can be used to look for opportunities to innovate. For example, can it be used to identify an unmet demand in a marketplace?

AI can help to generate new ideas, enable disruptive business models and enhance many types of product and services. Furthermore, there is a place within the innovation cycle for creativity in the usual artistic sense and AI is already contributing to these activities as well. I discuss this in more detail later in this chapter.

The number and breadth of AI announcements can be overwhelming so I take a systematic approach to thinking through which innovations might apply to specific business contexts.

For many of us, the organisation for which we work gives us boundaries. We might have a great idea but it really does not fit our organisation. To turn the subject on its head, I look at an approach for identifying innovations within a constrained business context. Most organisations have plenty of problems that need imaginative solutions but they are not blank canvases. I use a generally acceptable definition of innovation to look at business models, markets, products and services. To make the discussion more concrete, I use an example of a business with a few typical business challenges and I suggest an approach to finding the most promising innovation that would work within normal project constraints.

To fuel some further ideas, I look at combinations of technologies. That is, AI working in combination with other technologies that will allow a step change in potential benefits. This, in combination with a comparison between sectors, gives a range of ideas, concepts and solutions that can apply to your organisation. I back up each combination with an example from around the world.

Finally, I look at some of the ways AI is being used in the creative industries for generating art, music, designs and sketches. These capabilities could soon extend your products or service but even if this is not a possibility, the field of AI in the creative arts is interesting for anyone who wants to see where innovations in 5 or 10 years will come from. New visualisations of products and possibly even ways of thinking about services are likely to emerge.

Before we begin looking at specific business scenarios, it is worth pausing to ask why AI is a catalyst for so much innovation. The best answer is that it is a so-called 'general purpose technology' that ranks alongside the advent of the digital computer, and World Wide Web, as written about in 'The impact of artificial intelligence on innovation' published by the National Bureau of Economic Research in 2018 (Cockburn et al., 2018). This has led to the expectation that it will impact many aspects of our business and personal lives to the same degree as the personal computer, mobile phone or the web, and that AI in turn will bring about a faster pace of change because of four key factors:

- Funding: the capital markets are now alive to AI's capability, so funds have been diverted to drive further research. There are many announcements and estimates of the amount of money being poured into the industry. According to one such study, the MoneyTree™ report published by PwC CB Insights (PwC CB Insights, 2020), startups' ambitious AI-based new product development was driving AI-related investment. The report estimated $16.5 billion was raised in 2019 in 695 deals.

- Technology: deep learning is now key to eye-catching developments like autonomous cars that connect with a wide population of opinion formers. It is no longer in the laboratories classifying pictures of cats.

- Innovation: AI is a tool for innovation in its own right. It can be thought of as an invention that is a method of invention so is difficult to dismiss or pigeonhole as 'not for us'.

- Ubiquity: the greater ubiquity in our everyday lives raises awareness among private and public sector decision-makers.

These drivers and others are leading to a snowball effect and the expectation that AI can address some of society's biggest issues: managing an aging population; the transition to low carbon energy; better governance; and better quality education. Not only can AI contribute to the solution to some of these long-term problems, it can also contribute to the process of innovation itself. That is, identifying and selecting ideas that will solve a problem. This is where I start the discussion in this chapter: how to harness AI to address identifiable wants and needs. I then look at a typical innovation cycle within a business and see how AI is contributing to different business models, processes, products and changing markets.

In many cases, the greatest opportunities for short-term innovation come from combining AI technology with other existing facilities or processes. A discipline that is moving at lightning pace is video games technology. AI is already part of many games and, in this chapter, we explore how some of the platforms and toolkits can be used in the world of corporate IT.

Research shows how AI can then go further and contribute to the creative process. Experimental research in art, writing and abstract reasoning show how AI can enhance the human capacity to look at the world in a different way and, in doing so, open up new possibilities. How this research can be harnessed in business is a leading-edge topic. Maybe readers of this book will consult some of the references and go on to pioneer new solutions and ideas. In the meantime, I am going to start by looking at AI-enhanced innovation in a corporate environment.

APPLYING AI TO INNOVATION IN YOUR BUSINESS

Let's start with defining what we mean by innovation in a corporate environment. This definition from TechTarget (TechTarget, n.d.) is practical and to the point so I have chosen to use it for this chapter:

> Business innovation is an organisation's process for introducing new ideas, workflows, methodologies, services or products. The cycle is often broken down into four parts. It starts with articulating ideas around key areas (business models, marketing, process, products and service).

So, I will start with a discussion about generating ideas in the first place, then look at how AI can contribute to innovation of business models, markets, processes and finally products and services.

Generating ideas

Business innovation of any type usually falls into one of two categories: new ways of dealing with existing requirements; or ways to satisfy an unrecognised need.

AI can help by looking at customer behaviour in ways that are very difficult with a human mind because we cannot see the patterns in very large amounts of data. If you have access to large enough datasets then you can, potentially uniquely, find customer behaviour patterns that will allow you to change your business model, marketing, processes, products or services.

Here are five ways that AI and deep learning can help you to spark ideas in your organisation.

- Finding the opportunity in a mass of data to improve something: one example is to use deep learning to spot how your customers are behaving over large populations or over long periods of time. Can you detect when a customer will defect to the competition? Can you understand the patterns of behaviour before they adopt or abandon your product or service?

- Product usage: if you collect feedback on the way that products are used, for example white goods, energy products, or anything online, then what is it telling you about how the product or customer experience can radically change?

- Abstract reasoning: this is still a research topic in AI but the discussion in this chapter on how deep learning can approach abstract learning shows that associating concepts and linking ideas can lead to new approaches for existing problems.

- Combining AI with other solutions: these are often other information processing solutions but some of the most exciting do span into the physical world as well – they are phygital.

- Combining AI from different fields: gaming technology is leading the way in many aspects of AI. How many of these techniques can be applied in your business? How many can improve your employees' experience?

These points hint at innovation approaches, they do not suggest an innovation that will improve the customer proposition or go to meet an unrecognised need. The following sections give some ideas that can be immediately put to use in organisations today but should be read in combination with the sections that cover how AI is being applied to the creative industries and abstract thinking.

> Visual representations of customer propositions are becoming more important and use of AI in this field is evolving rapidly.

Business models

There are many examples of innovative and disruptive business models. AirBnB, Rightmove, Peleton and Uber are all good mainstream examples. Many of these organisations were able to disrupt existing industries because of the advent of the World Wide Web in conjunction with smartphones. In fact, there are now literally thousands of companies that have introduced a new business model into their own sectors – and that change has been made possible by new communications technology.

It is generally accepted that these new models were enabled by a combination of the following factors, highlighted many years ago by Lee in his 2001 paper 'An analytical framework for evaluating e-commerce business models and strategies' (Lee, 2001):

- reduction in transaction costs;
- transfer of risk;
- changing trust balance;
- untapped capacity;
- disintermediation;
- transparency;
- real-world monitoring through the IoT.

When Lee outlined the seven points in his paper in 2001 he could see these factors would impact business models. However, it wasn't until many years later that the disruptive businesses mentioned above emerged.

One of the points that I make in this book is that the technology shift due to AI is every bit as disruptive as the web and smartphones and arguably speeds up the pace of disruption.

Here, I look at how AI adds a step change into the factors that disrupt business models with some examples that are already emerging. Many new models will emerge but from the evidence already available there are at least four types of models that are actively enabled by AI:

- micro outsourcing;
- changing commercial boundaries;

- changing physical boundaries;
- high-value technical advances.

I look at each of these models in turn and give examples of organisations that are exploiting the change.

Micro outsourcing

Transaction costs, untapped capacity, reduction in production costs; these three factors led to the viability of externalising specialised but small-volume services. Because of the smaller volumes than are normally associated with outsourcing this is sometimes called micro outsourcing. AI will accelerate this trend because some types of micro outsourcing can be made much more efficient, for example by automating narrow services that are supplied to many organisations.

An example is Ampere music that uses AI to generate a soundtrack for videos. Providing these services at a feasible cost has been difficult in the past but now AI can be used to both understand the brief, in this case the type and style of music overlay, say, a corporate video, and then produce the soundtrack. This is a good example of a service that is quite difficult to source in small volumes for a typical business, but can be supplied to multiple organisations at a fraction of the price of using an internal team.

Extending the function of an intelligent home speaker/assistant to take account of the sound emitted by your home's smoke alarm or the sound of breaking glass is another example. This is where specialist monitoring equipment and services such as alarm systems are being disrupted by not only reduced transaction costs, but also replacement of relatively low-volume parts by a general device (the smart speaker), thereby greatly reducing the cost of production.

The ability to reduce the risk or cost of a particular process due to the investment in AI is evidenced by Xihelp Ltd. This company produces a robotic fruit picker. The mechanism for picking fruit and the AI that controls it are closely integrated. The company can contain the risk of using the machine in a glasshouse setting and reduce the cost of the process of picking and placing the fruit in punnets. The company offers to outsource this process for farmers (https://xihelm.com), not by providing the equipment but by outsourcing the 'fruit-to-punnet' process.

A further example emerges from 3D printing. Although not an AI technology in its own right, there are now services that allow you to upload a 2D photograph. AI is then applied to 'guess' the 3D shape of the subject from the hints in the 2D image. Depending on the level of skill needed to control and optimise the 3D rendering, it may be that this work is completed by a 3D printing shop, or completely in-sourced because it is the best way to get from a photograph to a physical prototype through your own 3D printing equipment. This is using technology powered by AI to create new services and commercial models – something that was not easy to do before its widespread use.

Although these services are mostly based on information with some impact on the physical world, it is reasonable to expect this balance to change as more general purpose intelligent assistants become available.

Changing commercial boundaries

Almost every commercial boundary between a company and its stakeholders – customers, suppliers, regulators – has been challenged by the disruptive models of the last 20 years and I would argue that the AI revolution will increase the pace of that disruption in the future.

Between customers and companies it seems likely that customers will demand a better service before they commit to a purchase or a brand. Competitors will find ways to provide attractive services at very low cost using AI. These services may require a 'freemium' offer as we see in the software industry when a product or service is offered without charge for a period of time to allow customers to try the product before paying for it.

Continuing the thoughts about micro outsourcing, the relationship with suppliers will change in a similar way. On the other hand, the efficiency gained through your deployment of AI might mean that it is more beneficial to bring a service that has been outsourced in-house.

The services that are currently outsourced will be candidates for in-sourcing. There is no point in paying for a large off-shore contact centre when an automated customer interface can handle the service requests better and at a reduced cost.

Changing physical boundaries

As AI impacts the physical world, the current physical boundaries around an organisation will be challenged. Sometimes it will continue to make sense to manufacture in large factories. In other cases manufacturing close to the demand will become feasible and be more efficient. If we treat house building as a form of manufacturing, we have a great example of changing physical boundaries. There are many projects around the world (CyBe, Icon) which show that 3D printing can be applied to domestic house building and industrial construction projects. Proponents of these projects say that there are three advantages:

- A common design can be used for many implementations of the same building.
- A variety of expensive low-volume parts can be replaced with standard blocks or a specific type of fluid concrete that can be built up in layers.
- Most of the build is mechanised and the results matched back to the specification.

The economics of construction can be changed dramatically using these three measures. It has been hundreds of years since the cost of manufacture for transportable goods was minimised by using factories that delivered at scale, but the model could not be applied to construction. In this case, 3D printing can deliver some of those efficiency advantages without being constrained by factory walls.

Equally, organisations will be able to provide a service where the demand is needed, away from their main or regional offices. An example is how some local authorities, due to financial constraints, are using their libraries, community centres or job centres to provide online services to clients that might not have access to the internet at home. The councils provide kiosks equipped with PCs to allow customers to access services online. The customers can ask questions about their services that are then answered automatically by a chatbot and, if necessary, passed to an expert, who might be available in person at that location or working remotely. In this way, the customer gets a better service at a location that is convenient for them while the council makes maximum use of its expert resources wherever they are located. This has been particularly useful during the COVID-19 pandemic when customers have been able to pop in to their nearest facility to access services online and the council's experts have been able to continue to offer help and advice while working in their preferred work locations with services partially automated or augmented by chatbots.

High-value technical advances

The most disruptive models will be those with a value proposition that is a leap in the eyes of the customer. Typically these will be the large-scale moon-shot plays and there will probably be a relatively small number of organisations that end up with commercially transformative products. We know that the likes of self-driving cars, user interfaces for computers and personal service platforms will be continually enhanced. They will catch the headlines and a small number of organisations will probably transform the way we live using applications of AI that may not have even been imagined yet. However, the bigger effect on our lives will come from how AI impacts almost every organisation. To visualise this, the following sections describe innovation within a corporate context – markets, processes, products – and then lead on to the fascinating area of AI in the creative industries.

Markets

Financial markets may be the first place that the implications of AI become clear. The rise and rise of algorithmic trading in the financial markets is an interesting indicator. As Purba Mukerji observes (Mukerji, 2019), algorithmic trading started as a minor activity in the 1990s but recently has accounted for 85 per cent of trades in US markets. The algorithms have changed over this period of time and the degree of intelligence has increased with every advancing year. It is fair to conclude that in the most competitive of markets, large organisations are putting their trust in these algorithms to judge price and timing better than skilled traders. So if AI can make such a big impact on financial markets, how will it affect other markets?

Maybe it is reasonable to expect that if capital markets provide the environment for the earliest adoption of technologies then retail financial markets are a close second. The rise of robo-advisors is an interesting example. These systems are relatively simple, and regulation, thankfully, means they cannot be unconstrained. Nonetheless, the types of predictive personal shopper that may be a feature of other retail markets may make more of an appearance in the future too.

Any market where decisions by market actors can be improved with more transparent information or better predictions can be disrupted, such as the travel or retail industries where information about prices and offers is widely available. When you consider innovation in the market that your organisation operates in, price discovery, better prediction of supply and demand and difficult to anticipate disruption are factors to consider.

Processes

This book has many examples of processes that are totally changed through AI: application processes, fulfilment processes, customer service processes and so on. One example that is apt to discuss in this context is AI's role in process innovation. I believe the following examples illustrate this point well.

A contact centre operator achieved major benefits rapidly from application of AI in process optimisation. All processes involve steps sequenced in time. In large organisations with many people, these process steps can vary as staff adopt different practices over time. To understand the level of variations in what should be standardised processes, the contact centre operator uses a desktop mining tool to discover exactly what the processes are and how long each step takes. It then uses the information to drive process improvements, firstly through a top–down approach that takes best practice and codifies it for everyone, using technology to automate some steps in the target group of processes, and secondly, bottom–up process improvement through training, measurement and successive refinement. Without the AI tool it would be infeasible to capture, collect and analyse all the process-related information in a way that shows the patterns and the opportunities for improvement and process modernisation.

Calderdale Council provides another example in the case study in Chapter 6. Here the business driver was to increase the levels of self-service; a strategy that delivered more benefits than expected because of the COVID-19 pandemic that increased demand for online services. The AI front-end that was added to the council's website enables the customer to start a conversation that allows the right expert or advisor to be consulted should it be necessary. The conversational interface answers questions first and fully whenever possible but if the case needs to be handled by an expert the routing and summary information means the right advisor is brought into the conversation wherever they may be and with the history of the case at least partly provided to them.

I believe that it is possible to characterise the impact of AI on process innovation as follows:

- process discovery/process mining to identify the optimisation needed;
- incremental automation (e.g. image and voice processing);
- outsourcing replacement (e.g. music for videos);
- process intelligence (virtual assistants, predictive answers);
- physical process changes (e.g. pothole filling, simple deliveries, social care service platforms);
- self-mending processes (automated exception handling).

Examples of each of these types of process innovation are provided in this book and can be translated into many other commercial and public sector settings.

Products and services

Innovative AI products are being invented every day. From the 'Generating ideas' section at the start of this chapter, these products can be classified as either as a moon-shot technology leap or as an AI increment on existing proven products. In this section I concentrate on the second category, because it is more relevant to the majority of organisations.

To enhance your product, you can consider using one of the areas where AI has proven itself in a commercial setting:

- NLP;
- analysis and prediction;
- image recognition and classification;
- process optimisation and exception handling;
- extensions to the physical environment;
- gaming technology.

You may then be able to use AI with existing technology that you have already deployed or apply it in a different way to gain improvements. The following section gives several examples and shows how selecting complementary solutions can be effective.

AI in combination with other solutions

In many business settings the ideas with the best returns will probably be based on AI in combination with other technologies. With this notion in mind, here is a list of combinations of technologies that are getting traction in projects and organisations around the world.

AI in the physical world
Vacuum cleaners, lawn mowers and pool cleaners have been automated for some time with increasing intelligence built in. The universal butler is still some way off. What will be the next 'killer app' in the physical robot world? In this section I explore a few ideas that hint at what is to come.

The need for additional resources in adult social care is well documented. Kind, empathetic people are needed but there are not enough of them. If time-consuming repetitive tasks can be taken off their work schedule then they have more time to provide empathy and comfort. In Japan this idea is better accepted than in many other cultures where they have used service robots for helping rather than replacing caring human beings. Their approach broadly is to use the service robots to do the fetching, carrying and other routine tasks to leave the carers to spend more time with people.

Closer to home here in the UK, one example of the kind of projects that are advancing applications of AI in social care is Care at Home using Intelligent Robotic Omni-function Nodes (CHIRON) (CHIRON, 2018). This was a project funded by Innovate UK, to design care robotics that ensure dignity, independence and choice. It ran from 2016 to 2018 and resulted in a prototype modular robotic system called JUVA, that was not one robot but a set of modular intelligent solutions, positioned in different places around the home to help people with tasks throughout the day.

Service robots for local deliveries are well established with many small and large area trials. Service robots for domestic use are less well advanced.

It is reasonable to extrapolate the use of digital assistants with existing, though not widely used, service robots. Maybe starting with just monitoring (e.g. Alexa Guard) then information provision, such as reminders for medication with light-touch monitoring, then progressively more useful physical assistance.

Digital prototyping is used to visualise new products, buildings and landscapes. For some types of products, and even buildings, once they can be visualised they can be built using advances in 3D printing.

Innovation in these areas will continue apace because they are the subject of mainstream research investment. In the meantime, there will be incremental innovation by combining existing technologies with AI.

AI and process automation

IA/IPA including intelligent document management have been the route to large-scale savings in many organisations. There is an increasing role for more AI to combine with these technologies.

Opportunities exist with software solutions today to capture information about a process, and re-engineer it, improve it through conversational interfaces, embedded AI within data entry forms and then a combination of AI with RPA technologies or application programming interfaces (APIs). Chapter 4 discusses many technologies that enable process automation.

Just by examining the case studies in this book it is easy to see how a business process can be re-engineered. The high-cost areas of the process can then be further automated using NLP and conversational interfaces and continually improving exception handling. The continually improving exception handling evolves into an adaptive process. If an exception occurs more than 10 per cent of the time then it is generally accepted that it is a path through the process and not an exception. A common area in which these exceptions occur is the integration between systems. AI has a specific role in these technologies to change the task from 'transfer this record that represents a service request into back office system A' to 'a customer has reported a potential fault with these characteristics' and the AI then learns how that situation should be represented in the back office system and the limitations of the import mechanism, be it through an API, RPA engine or batch record imports.

The result would be a set of processes that are continually evolving to engineer out exceptions with the AI learning from the process.

AI and the Internet of Things

For many business processes there is an input or output that impacts the direct physical world. Continuing the example from the previous section, which discussed aspects of a fault handling process, the fault could have been directly reported by a device in the field. This is an example of the IoT. It may also be that manufacturers choose to make their error displays such that an image contains all the information needed to process the fault. The image is forwarded by the customer or person who inspects the machine and it is recognised and parsed by AI to initiate the process of resolving the fault.

Other processes would be initiated by physical devices, for example when an alarm goes off to indicate a break in a part of a physical intrusion detection system. Another example is reactive and planned maintenance for connected plant and machinery, when automated testing of machinery is activated based on a daily schedule at the end of the day.

In the home, these processes are likely to be oriented around a small number of trusted devices, making those devices more important.

AI and augmented desktops

For many typical office-based roles, including knowledge workers, designers, sales agents and customer service agents, there are AI helpers that work with the combination of systems that are already in use and assist the employee. Examples are best answers, next-best-action recommendation engines and cross-sell and up-sell recommendation engines. Some of these systems are proprietary and part of, for example, customer relationship management systems.

AI and conversational forms

Organisations ask customers to complete complex online forms. Unfortunately the more complex the form, the more likely a customer is to make a mistake. For example, when claiming Child and Working Tax Credits in the UK, errors account for over four per cent overpayment (HM Revenue and Customs, 2020), which represents more than £1 billion per year. To enhance accuracy a conversational interface can help, particularly if there is specialist language or terms involved.

AI and application development platforms

Organisations that create application development tools are actively introducing AI into their products. Although it is not the focus of this book, which is aimed at business use of AI rather than its technical uses, it is interesting to see how this field is developing because it shows some of the future paths that will influence the use of AI in business:

- AI created systems: these systems are created from the ground up starting with requirements through design, test and deployment and ongoing improvements. Currently this approach is only feasible for relatively simple systems such as websites with well characterised functionality. An example is Aida from Bookmark. This AI provides an initial website from a relatively simple specification. The site then improves itself with use (https://www.bookmark.com/).

- There are many tools that help the developer with an aspect of the tooling. Examples are auto-complete tools such as Kite for Python.

- There are also tools that attempt to automatically fix code that is causing errors to be reported such as DrRepair (https://worksheets.codalab.org/worksheets/0x01 838644724a433c932bef4cb5c42fbd).

As these tools rapidly develop and converge it is reasonable to extrapolate a bit further and see that the process of specification will become streamlined through a conversation or dialogue that introduces enough visual and time-based elements to be able to assemble more complex systems. A machine-generated specification producing the working product is within the future capabilities of many current platforms.

AI in games platforms and product innovation

Games creators are constantly pushing the boundaries of current technology and that includes AI. Many would argue that the behaviour of so-called non-player characters

(NPCs) is a stringent test for AI in other applications. There is a clear crossover between that aspect of games technology and the virtual assistant toolkits that are currently mainstream in the corporate world. There are companies that already target this point of need, combining the AI of a chatbot with the avatar rendering of a games engine (example: https://www.pinscreen.com/virtualassistant).

Games environments are also being used to provide test-beds for AI of different types. A paper by DeepMind called 'Using unity to help solve intelligence' (DeepMind, 2020) describes a joint initiative with the widely used Unity gaming platform. A toolkit called ML-Agents allows NPCs to be trained rather than scripted or coded. That in turn puts an emphasis on making the gaming environment a sufficient simulation to train the avatar. This has a parallel with the way, for example, that autonomous car makers are using simulation environments to ensure that their AI is well trained before it sees a test track.

So the worlds of video games and corporate IT are already merging and the underlying technology is already in place. The right customer experience will combine with cultural acceptance and business need to provide disruptive products in this area.

AI and enterprise resource planning

Vendors of ERP solutions, such as Oracle and SAP, are adding more AI capabilities to their products. This is important because ERP software is very widely adopted across industries. Consequently, there is more and more AI being deployed across organisations. ERP systems can be broad, both in terms of the business functions used and adoption within an organisation. There will be many potential uses of AI.

For the modules that are used by a large number of occasional users (e.g. expenses, employee benefits, ad hoc procurement) then conversational interfaces either using text or voice will most likely be of benefit.

Of more profound impact will be the use of AI to reduce the number of process-related exceptions or to automatically handle exceptions when they do arise. Invoice and order exceptions in large organisations can easily run at 10 to 20 per cent. Reducing this rate both reduces cost and probably improves overall data quality. It is that data quality which leads to possibly the most important role of AI in ERP and that is to use the very rich data resources to build better predictions and to identify anomalies in the data that tend to get masked using standard aggregation techniques.

AI and IT service delivery

Due to its technical nature, IT service delivery has been an early adopter of AI. In fact, the very specialised field of intrusion detection and monitoring for cybersecurity was one of the earliest areas to use AI to try to spot unusual patterns of use. There are many other uses of AI within IT service delivery, for example detecting potential system failures from past performance or proactively and automatically managing infrastructure to avoid computing performance issues.

In the context of innovation, the degree to which AI is used in IT infrastructure management is increasing and there is even talk of self-aware infrastructures that effectively look after themselves through means such as pattern matching, root cause analysis, event correlation and forecasting as part of managing operations. This is often referred to as AI for IT operations or AIOps for short. Examples include monitoring demand for services and spinning up or decommissioning servers in the cloud as needed, or preventing and countering cyberattacks.

AI AND CREATIVITY

In this book I concentrate on the business applications of AI and so this short sortie into the world of the creative arts is just to complement the use of AI in other areas. Here are a few examples that show how AI can enhance or change the process of creating paintings and music. Then I briefly discuss the application of AI to abstract reasoning.

Painting/imagery

In 2018, an AI-generated painting found some coverage in the press when it achieved a six-figure sale value at auction.

A video of the portrait of Edmond Belamy shows the AI building up from sketches or abstract shapes to a portrait that can be seen on YouTube https://www.youtube.com/watch?v=Gka250M4wGk

Of more direct applicability for business is the ability to take a sketch and turn it into an artist's impression of, say, a building. Furthermore, the image can then be given the artistic style that you want. Although most systems of this kind are in their early prototype stage, it is clear that the ability to turn a rough sketch into an image and then a design is not far away.

Music

Creating music has been a field of AI for several decades. One example of a company that is solving a particular business problem is Ampere Music. Their web-based facility provides a way to create unique backing music for videos. The style and type of music can be selected and then timings matched to the video. This is an otherwise awkward facility to create without specialist skills so is a use of creative AI that immediately applies to business (www.ampermusic.com).

The experiment for open.ai that uses the GPT2 architecture of neural network to compose music is interesting. There are some very compelling examples on the open.ai MuseNet site (https://openai.com/blog/musenet/).

There are many more AI music composers that range from the simple to those that require professional music knowledge and are designed to enhance the skills of accomplished composers. For those with a particular interest in this field there is an annual AI song contest (https://www.aisongcontest.com/) during which teams compete for the best composition. Most AI competitions are taken very seriously but this one is a bit more light-hearted.

Abstract problem solving

Finally in this section I briefly discuss how AI is moving into abstract problem solving. That is, away from closed questions like 'is this an image of a cat?' to the types of problems with a desired answer but no clear way of structuring the path to the result. An example might be, 'When should I launch product A?' There is no right answer, but neural networks can be used to try to infer a way of getting to an answer and then provide an explanation of their method.

This is a research field but may apply to business very soon with the level of effort that is being applied. The architecture in a paper by a team at DeepMind, 'Measuring abstract reasoning in neural networks' (Lillicrap, 2018), shows one approach that can be applied directly.

In this example a specific class of abstract problem was chosen. The neural networks were set up to try to infer the way that a pattern was derived from other patterns. There was always a way of deriving the answer in these examples and although the paper starts with a reference to one of Einstein's thought experiments, it is not clear how the technique could be generalised that far. But it is clear how it could answer 'Is there a best time to launch product A?' or even, given past history, 'Should I launch product A or C next?'

Neural networks that can provide directly commercially useful abstract thinking are still in the research laboratories. The field is mentioned here because it adds to the overall picture and hints at the future direction where decision-support systems will take a significant leap forward.

THE AI FOUNTAIN

So far I have covered AI for innovation and how it can go across intersections of the digital and physical worlds, in business as well as arts and creativity. In the next chapter I cover AI for efficiency.

To bring all these threads together, I have created a visualisation of AI as a fountain from which springs the potential for enhanced human work in the digital and physical worlds, and smarter machines. It will also help with skills and capabilities, for example providing data for reasoning and decision-making, and different approaches to design and innovation, as well as creativity. AI is already augmenting some human work and activity, and, as it advances, it will be enabling autonomic systems that in time will lead to autonomous enterprises. This is where humans will augment AI to ensure the quality of its operations, its governance and ethical, human-centric behaviour.

These ideas are captured in Figure 3.1.

Figure 3.1 The AI fountain from which springs the potential for augmented human work in the digital and physical worlds, and smarter machines

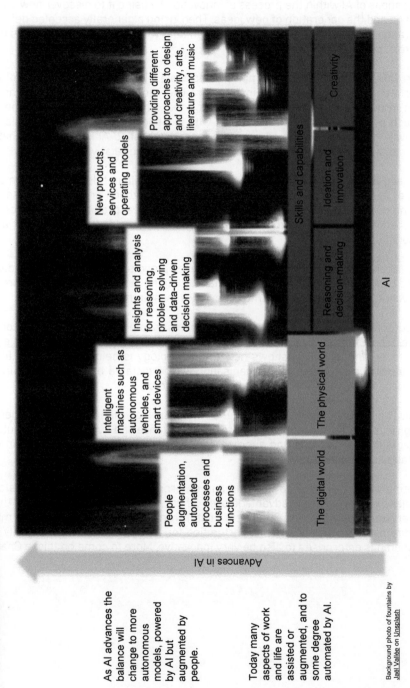

As AI advances the balance will change to more autonomous models, powered by AI but augmented by people.

Today many aspects of work and life are assisted or augmented, and to some degree automated by AI.

SUMMARY

In this chapter I examined the role of AI in business innovation. I started by looking at applications of AI within the process of innovation by using it to discover new customer demand and the generation of new ideas. Then, using a generally accepted definition of innovation in business, I explored how AI can help with innovation in business models, markets, products and services.

To provide as many specific examples as possible, I looked at combinations of AI with other technologies. These combinations are likely to contribute the most immediate gains in many organisations. In particular, I looked at combining a common use of AI, such as NLP or image classification, with existing technologies. The availability of relatively mature toolkits in some of the more established AI fields means that these projects that combine technologies can be implemented relatively simply.

The need to focus on the practical and achievable should not detract from some of the uses of AI that are more far-reaching. Although I only touch briefly on the use of AI in art and music, the very fact that there are now practical products and services being launched in that field is profound. Even more fundamental is the use of AI for abstract reasoning.

If the regulators stay ahead of the technical developments, and the ethical considerations raised by AI are well and truly taken in hand, then the increasing power and breadth of the technology can help with some of society's most intractable issues.

In a corporate context, there are some ideas in this chapter that should at least contribute to the debate in many organisations. Each idea or solution put forward has an example referenced and usually it shows how the technology is being used in real life. How radical you want to be in your organisation will be dictated by your own environment but I hope there are some ideas here you can build on.

Finally, I introduced the AI fountain out of which springs many new developments that will give us a variety of capabilities – from AI assistance and augmentation to autonomic systems that we will use and augment to ensure their relevance and human-centric operation and behaviour.

Relating all of this back to autonomous enterprises, many early adopters of AI in business will have a huge advantage over others simply because of the data that they will accumulate from their intelligent digital transactions. The data can be mined to identify patterns that point to opportunities for innovation. Therefore, I fully expect autonomous enterprises to also be very innovative. More to come on this in Chapter 9.

4   AI FOR EFFICIENCY

In this chapter I discuss uses of AI to boost business efficiency, an objective that leading organisations strive for as part of ambitious continuous improvement programmes that increasingly include automating processes. These in turn are leading to the evolution of organisations into autonomous enterprises where the bulk of high-volume, repetitive and transactional work as well as many customer interactions and decision-making tasks will be done by machines. In turn, humans will only get involved in supervision of the work, guiding the software robots and handling exceptions or in customer interactions where empathy is needed. They will continue to develop, maintain and supervise the automations.

Increasing efficiency year-on-year is a major driver for investment in technology and for many projects that enterprises undertake. Much of the effort has been focused on improving the front line of operations where interactions with customers happen, as well as line of business and administrative processes. In recent years employee engagement has also come into sharper focus, rising as an enterprise priority. This is driven by a shortage of skills and the costs of hiring.

Applications of intelligent technology will help by augmenting human workers, enabling them to work faster and better while reducing their repetitive and uninteresting workload. For example, AI can help contact centre agents by delivering information to them in real time, in the context of the conversation that they are having with customers, to help them answer questions faster and better, or walk them through the next steps of a complicated process. This is what I call human augmentation; where technology helps staff with their daily tasks, to increase productivity, job satisfaction levels and consequently reducing staff attrition and costs of hiring and skills development.

The technology can learn to augment humans in different ways, for example by following the work of subject matter experts and learning how they deal with processes and exceptions, or by analysing data about interactions, such as how calls were handled on similar subjects in the past, or by using a custom-built knowledge-base.

AI can greatly help enterprises in their search for efficiency in many different ways. In this chapter, I first provide a few examples of AI for efficiency in settings other than business processes. Then, I focus on enablers of the autonomous enterprise and its automated business functions, I delve into a group of technologies that can deliver efficiency in the context of enterprise business processes and knowledge work automation. These are a set of technologies that combine to provide IA and I provide an introduction to each of them and give examples of their applications.

BRINGING AI FOR EFFICIENCY TO LIFE

The case studies in Chapters 5 to 8 provide real life examples of AI enabling process efficiency. These are from a diverse group of organisations that vary in size and nature of work. There are many other examples too and I cover a number of them in the following sections.

AI to improve decision-making

AI can be used to improve decision-making. The ability to make decisions based on hard facts is always important but particularly so in times of uncertainty and increased business complexity. One example that is very apt in the pandemic, when supply chains have been disrupted due to illness in the workforce, is ensuring the flow of supplies to where they are needed. Some organisations are using advanced analytics powered by machine learning to identify where in their vast network of warehouses they might have surplus supplies. These can then be diverted to where there is a shortage to assure business continuity in the affected locations.

Another example is AI helping physicians make better decisions by analysing the results of X-rays and computerised tomography (CT) scans, as described in the case study in Chapter 7, on Royal Berkshire NHS Foundation Trust (RBFT) improving stroke care. The software deployed at RBFT helps emergency doctors to better diagnose the damage caused by stroke. This, combined with other steps to make the care process more efficient, is improving overall patient outcomes, particularly for those who present out of hours when emergency doctors may not be able to reach specialists to consult them nor have experienced radiologists available to diagnose the extent of the damage shown in the scans. The technology not only identifies the likely locations of brain clots shown by the scan, it also allows the images to be quickly shared with specialists who are not on site, on their mobiles or other hand-held devices. This enables emergency doctors to consult the specialists remotely and decide the best course of treatment and referrals for the patient. This has resulted in patients receiving the appropriate treatment faster and has significantly improved the chances of them returning to normal life after their strokes.

Another example of AI in decision support is that covered in Chapter 8 – Wärtsilä's use of an intelligent configure price quote (CPQ) solution that helps their sales consultants to correctly configure complex power generation or ship engines to price and quote for. It also helps them to understand the impact of changing components and parts or an updated design on the chosen configuration and the pricing that must be recalculated.

AI for environmental efficiency

AI can help to reduce the impact of farming and heavy industrial operations on the environment. In farming, computer vision systems are emerging that identify weeds in fields of crops to allow weed killer to be sprayed only on them and not the actual crop, consequently generating savings on the amount of weed killer used. This reduces the quantity released into the environment and saves humans from having weed killer-covered produce.

Advanced analytics can make farming much more scientific; for example by analysing weather patterns and soil conditions to identify when to irrigate fields to reduce demand on dwindling water supplies in draught-prone areas.

In some heavy industries, advanced analytics are being used to manage and optimise power consumption. I have previously discussed the finding of the EU-funded FUDIPO (FUDIPO, 2016) project in Chapter 1, which found significant power savings could be achieved through intelligent controls in plants.

On the subject of power, AI can be used on the supply side of the market too to improve utilisation of green and renewable energy sources. One example is the UK's National Grid announcing (Shead, 2021) an investment in AI to understand shifting cloud patterns in order to predict how these might affect solar panels. When renewable supplies are uncertain, the National Grid has to keep fossil fuel-based supplies going to make up for any shortfalls. The AI will allow it to get a more accurate view of supplies from renewable sources, and consequently, be able to optimise its supplies and reduce its reliance on fossil fuels.

AI for efficiency of food production and supplies

There are other applications of AI that can make farming more scientific in order to produce better crop yields. Examples include analysis of weather patterns and soil conditions to predict the best time to plant seeds, how much fertiliser to use and when, and the optimum time to harvest crops.

In terms of the food supply chain, the use of advanced analytics can help organisations plan their supply delivery routes better, to find the optimum routes. This could be used for any part of the delivery network, from planning global shipping routes to local door-to-door deliveries.

Improving health and social care

In healthcare, intelligent health monitoring of patients can be used to predict and prevent problems. In care for the elderly, IVAs can provide help and support to elderly people living alone through voice interactions. When connected to devices through the IoT they can also provide phygital services, such as switching home devices on and off on command or, according to schedules, provide physical security and alerting systems around the home, as well as checking the well-being of the elderly resident. The latter can be done by detecting changes in the patterns of movement around the home. A lack of movement might indicate a fall or other health problems and a relative or carer could be alerted to check on the elderly resident.

AI for business efficiency

AI for business efficiency is a major enabler of the autonomous enterprise. There is much AI that is already embedded in IA solutions and they are key to building the autonomous enterprise. Accordingly, in the rest of this chapter I focus on IA technologies that provide the means of achieving more efficiency in business operations.

WHAT IS INTELLIGENT AUTOMATION?

IA is a category in the field of technology that covers a range of solutions that help organisations automate business processes that would otherwise be done manually. In their book *Intelligent Automation*, Bornet, Barkin and Wirtz (2020) define it as:

> IA, also called Hyperautomation, is a concept leveraging a new generation of software-based automation. It combines methods (for example process design, implementation and project delivery, and change management) and technologies (for example machine learning, computer vision, NLP, APIs, RPA) to execute business processes automatically on behalf of knowledge-workers. This automation is achieved by mimicking the capabilities that knowledge workers use in performing their work activities (for example language, vision, execution, and thinking and learning).

I covered many of the technologies mentioned in the definition in Chapter 2 and will expand on them later in this chapter. Other definitions are provided in the Glossary. In this section I focus on automation of business processes.

The processes that are automated using IA often include transactions and data that go across enterprise systems. When not automated, some of these involve people cutting and pasting data from one window on their desktop generated by one business application to another, and in doing so undertaking what is known as swivel chair integration. The bulk of these are transactions involving the handling of structured data, such as names, numbers and prices – the kind of data that can be processed by non-IA tools, for example classic RPA. However, some processes require documents to be checked for references, content in emails and text in chat messages as well as voice calls. These could involve checking a PO, reading a letter of complaint from a customer, details of instructions in a message sent by a banking client and so on. Where language, voice, text and images are involved we are dealing with unstructured data. To automate these types of tasks, intelligent software is needed with language-processing capabilities. In fact, intelligent software can handle all kinds of data – structured, semi-structured and unstructured – but they might not be able to connect to some legacy software applications in order to process the data; you might therefore need to connect to those using other technologies such as RPA.

IA is a software category that is made up of these types of technologies. Some are not inherently intelligent such as a lot of the current crop of RPA software, but many are including IDP, chatbots and IVAs.

By combining the components of IA you can automate almost any type of transactional process. At the moment the barrier is the level of complexity of the process and the law of diminishing returns. For example, the number of lines of code that you might need to write in order to create a robot to handle complex tasks can be prohibitive and the costs of developing and running big-ticket AI solutions could make the business case for such a project less than compelling.

Additionally, IA includes software solutions that use code injection to capture screen information to automate processes through the user interface of applications. These are typically used in contact centres to help automate some of the tasks that agents do.

Also increasingly coming under the umbrella of IA are orchestration software packages that help with the flow of controls between software robots (e.g. RPA) and intelligent solutions as well as machines and people and vice versa. While many RPA vendors have enhanced their built-in workflow and automation controls in their software packages, the third-party variety of orchestration software allows organisations to manage a mixed environment where automations are built on platforms provided by different IA vendors.

IA as a category is expanding and today is often used to refer to process mining and discovery software as well, even though many vendors in this field have been around for a while and quite separately from RPA that led to the creation of IA as a software category. These are included because they allow organisations to take a data-driven and analytical approach to identifying the processes that are good candidates for automation. In other words, they make it possible for organisations to take a data-driven approach to scaling up business process automation.

Figure 4.1 provides a pictorial representation of key components of IA and their most common features.

In the following sections, I describe the important components of IA, and provide examples of their use cases, their benefits and their challenges.

THE ROLE OF IA IN BUSINESS EFFICIENCY

In Chapter 1 I shared data from Everest Group's *Enterprise Intelligent Automation Adoption Maturity | Pinnacle Model™ Analysis* report (Everest Group, 2020) where 50 per cent of the Pinnacle enterprises had achieved cost savings of more than 60 per cent in the process area that the IA technology had been applied. The other 50 per cent reported savings of between 20 per cent and 60 per cent in the same context. Furthermore, out of the remaining group of 41 companies, 29 per cent had also achieved cost savings of over 60 per cent. These are significant figures that are driving automation. I provide more real life examples of the benefits of IA in the case studies in Chapters 5 to 8. The Siemens Global Business Services' example in Chapter 5 illustrates the efficiency savings particularly well; the company is saving on time, effort and costs by automating 70 per cent of its service ticket processing – with seven million tickets that its services generate, the resulting efficiency can be significant.

There are also many non-monetary benefits that can be realised from IA. I cover the key ones in the following sections.

Increased and flexible processing capacity

Automation increases the speed of processing and therefore more work can be done by the organisation, for example more cases processed. Accordingly, capacity to do business is increased. At times of high demand, the automated processes can be operated for longer every day to respond to the demand. Conversely, they can operate at reduced rates when demand is low, providing the enterprise with flexibility and agility.

Figure 4.1 Key components of IA

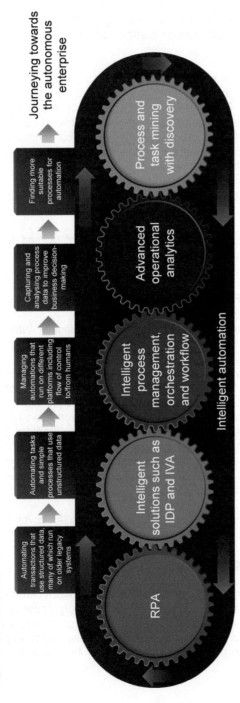

By combining IA technologies, more of each process can be automated and more types of business processes than any individual technology can do on its own.

Common features include:

- Some form of AI for example intelligent workflow and controls and/or NLP
- Low code with drag and drop features that make it easy to develop software robots and other types of automations
- Control panels, dashboards and reporting
- Ability to run on premises and on cloud
- Ability to capture process data, providing the basis for analytics, reporting and insights or runtime intelligence

Better quality of services

Process-related errors can lead to customer dissatisfaction and even reputational damage. When they occur they are costly to fix because of the duplicated effort required to not only fix the error but to redo the process and iron out any problems that the error has resulted in, for example claiming a refund back after it was sent to the wrong person. When fully tested, automation can reduce data errors, by copying and pasting data accurately, and consequently minimise the work required to fix any related issues.

Improved adherence to corporate and regulatory requirements and risk reduction

Automations follow the rules that humans give them and, therefore, increase the degree of standardisation of processes. When regulatory and corporate policy requirements are coded in the steps of the automated process, the level of adherence goes up. When data errors are reduced and requirements are coded into the body of the automated processes, risks are mitigated such as the risks of monetary fines and other sanctions due to failure to comply with regulations.

Improved employee engagement

If you automate the repetitive processes, you free staff to do the more interesting part of their daily routines such as handling complex cases. There are examples when work that was required to be done out of hours was automated, thus freeing staff from having to do night shifts. You can also augment work to help them do what they do better, with AI-powered technologies, for example next-best-action guidance and best answers in contact centres. All of these contribute towards more job satisfaction and increased employee engagement.

More data for business intelligence, decision support and innovation

Data provide business insights and you can program automations to capture and log business data for analysis. For example, reviewing operational data that get captured can show you better or innovative ways of handling customer interactions and improving online services, or increasing personalisation by matching customers to agents, based on their historical data and any affinity shown during past interactions. The same can help with better decision-making as well as increasing transparency of how and why decisions were made with regularly produced business intelligence reports.

Figure 4.2 summarises the benefits of IA.

IA TECHNOLOGIES

In this section I cover some of the main technologies that are used in IA for business process automation. You should think of these as building blocks to create an IA capability for your organisation. I have already mentioned these in the previous chapters of the book. Here, I look at them through an IA lens in a business context.

Figure 4.2 An overview of the benefits of IA

The benefits of IA

Faster and more standardised processes

Cost savings

Improved staff productivity and more engagement

Improved quality of processes and accuracy of data

Flexible capacity to deal with demand fluctuations and higher value processes

Embedded compliance and risk mitigation

Better customer experiences

More operational data for analysis, transparency, audit and reporting and to spot opportunities for innovation

IDP

IDP, also called intelligent content, refers to a group of software solutions that use AI to process enterprise content such as documents, forms, images and emails. IDP turns unstructured data in enterprise content into structured data using a string of capabilities including computer vision – technologies that allow machines to handle visual inputs, text analytics and NLP. The resulting structured data are then fed into other systems for further processing. The steps include image recognition or OCR, indexing and classification of the information, entity recognition and extraction that captures data from the information in the content, and validation against business rules, for example checking the format of a reference in a PO to ascertain its accuracy and compliance with procurement policies and standards. The solutions can then do further processing such as generating reports and insights, and pass the extracted data on to other systems.

Some IDP solutions are complemented with sentiment analysis that assesses the sentiment expressed by the words used in the content, and recommend further action, for example how angry a customer might be based on the words used in a complaint form and then making decisions on its urgency and priority.

IDP is useful to organisations that have to handle large numbers of documents every year, for example insurance companies handling claims that are accompanied by evidence such as photos, or banks doing KYC checks to open accounts for new clients or prior to approving loans and mortgages. The solutions capture key data from the documents submitted by the customer. If these are not in electronic form, they are scanned and digitised. After the information is captured the banks can verify the ID of the customer, checking all the information and comparing it with reference sources, for example address databases. They check the data for discrepancies that could indicate a problem.

IDP solutions for KYC typically finish the process in two ways: if no discrepancy is identified, they complete the process and create a report for a human to review. If an issue is identified they escalate it to a human worker as an exception and then learn from what the human does to resolve the issue and, consequently, enhance their skills.

There are many real life examples of banks that have significantly reduced their new customer onboarding processes from taking weeks to minutes. There are new and highly technology-enabled banks that use intelligent solutions to complete new clients' KYC processes in minutes compared with some established banks that, using legacy systems, take months. One example is a colleague of mine opening a new business account with one of the new breed of banks, using only his mobile phone while on a taxi ride in London. It didn't take him long to have his application approved and account opened. This was in contrast to his business partner's attempt to open an account with a major established UK bank that took many weeks.

The efficiency gain of onboarding clients in minutes compared with months can deliver cost savings, gain more customers and generate additional revenue. It can give the customers better experiences too as shown by the bank account opening example above.

Chatbots and IVAs

Chatbots and IVAs provide a way for people to interact with machines using human languages. They are powered by conversational AI based on NLP and its branches of natural language understanding (NLU) and natural language generation (NLG), which allow machines to understand and reply to written or voice-generated human languages (if they also have speech recognition capabilities).

You may well ask what the difference is between chatbots and IVAs. My way of differentiating between them is their levels of intelligence and built-in capabilities. With a chatbot, you are most likely to have a limited rules-based conversation, typically based on scripts, resulting in a reduced set of answers given by the chatbot. These are great for simple signposting, showing the user where to find more information. IVAs have more intelligence built into them – for example some of them have the ability to hold a conversation and remember the whole of it if you return to them a few days later. Chatbots are typically trained to handle conversations in one context but some IVAs can do more by their ability to switch context and still hold a reasonable conversation with you. They can understand intent, utterances and even sentiment. If you ask to be passed to a human agent, some IVAs are able to switch to become a guide to the agent that takes over the call. They do this by bringing the agent information that is relevant to the context of the conversation in real time.

Many of us have experienced the pain of having to wait on the phone for a contact centre agent to answer our call, while listening to horrible music and repeated recorded messages telling us how valuable our business is to the organisation. Bit by bit AI will help organisations to enhance their services to avoid these kinds of scenarios. They will also empower contact centre agents to be more productive leading to more efficiency and reduced costs for their operating organisations.

Anecdotally, one contact centre operator deployed a text-based chatbot to handle incoming hiring enquiries and saw the cost of recruitment reduce by more than 75 per cent per recruit over a six-month period. The same solution has allowed it to more than treble its capacity to handle incoming queries from candidates.

The same company has deployed intelligent tools to automate some of the chat channels that it runs for its clients. Firstly, it identified the opportunities for automation using intelligent desktop mining. It then automated the processes that were identified and recommended by the desktop mining tool. In its chat channel, in a matter of weeks, it saved in the region of $140,000 by deploying automation using NLP-based classification, and chatbots, resulting in only four per cent of staff needing to interact with clients via the channel.

According to research firm IDC (IDC, 2020a), European organisations spent $249.4 million in total on AI software in contact centre use cases in 2019. Furthermore, IDC reported that it expected European spending of $305.1 million in 2020, growing strongly in the coming years and rising to $916.6 million in 2024 (a compound annual growth rate of 30 per cent). It also believes that by 2023, rather than continue to move away from the voice channel, over 30 per cent of organisations will have added AI capability to their inbound call-handling environment (IDC, 2020b).

The case study in Chapter 6 provides a detailed look at how an English local authority, Calderdale Council, makes use of chatbots to improve its customer services and how it has helped the council deal with increased demand using a new services model.

RPA

In this section I cover RPA because it is core to the software category of IA, although typically it has no inherent intelligence of its own, except in some software that use computer vision to detect screen objects. RPA is rules-based with deterministic outcomes.

RPA describes a set of software solutions that integrate with other systems through their user interface (UI). This is because RPA mimics the steps that a human user would take to complete a task on a computer. This could be browsing the web to capture information from web pages for price comparisons for example, or logging in to an enterprise software system with credentials such as username and password to process a transaction, for example to update a customer address or transfer the details of an online order to an order processing system. By going through the UI, RPA connects to other systems in a way that is called non-invasive integration. This is because by going through the UI there is no need to make any changes to the systems that RPA connects to, and thus a lot of system integration work is avoided.

The word 'robot' refers to the software program that is developed by a programmer using the RPA software. These identify the required controls on the computer screen to mimic human users and work like them, for example to find a text field on the screen and enter data into it. This is where some RPA software use computer vision techniques, but many do not.

The use of the term 'robot' gives the impression of some level of machine intelligence but, as mentioned earlier in this section, this is misleading because these systems have little inherent intelligence. Most RPA solutions come with no machine learning capabilities and are able to only process structured data, the kind of data that you get in a database. They simply go through the instructions that the programmer has embedded in the robot code, step by step.

As time has gone by, RPA software vendors have integrated their solutions with intelligent products, allowing the robots to call routines from those intelligent products to be able to automate more processes. For example, before integration with intelligent solutions, a robot could be programmed to read only the structured data in an email – that is, the sender's name and email address, the subject field and the date and time in the email header. When integrated with an NLP solution, it can also read and make some sense of the unstructured data in the body of the email. Through this type of integration, these software robots are gaining intelligent skills.

The reason RPA vendors continue to extend the capabilities of their RPA is to be able to offer more functionality and to turn their basic RPA solutions into broad platforms that can automate more and more varieties of processes, voice or chat-based, and document-centric as well as transactional processes.

Some RPA solutions support APIs to allow the robots to connect to business systems in more ways than the UI. There are devotees of this model because going through the UI can be a fragile way of connecting to a business system. Changes such as an updated UI layout on an application or an unexpected pop-up window can lead to the robot failing to find the correct data field or object on the screen. The API approach is far more stable and I have had devoted users of RPA tell me that they connect through APIs where and when possible. That said, I believe the API approach means that the robots are no longer what RPA has to offer. They become more like the traditional system integration technology.

Styles of RPA
In the world of RPA you will come across some terms that define its style of operation. These include RPA itself, also known as unattended, attended or robotic desktop automation (RDA).

RPA or unattended automation   To some pundits RPA is all about unattended automation. That is when a robot is activated and runs according to predefined schedules or conditions, without a human having to activate it. For example, a robot can be run every night to update a system from multiple spreadsheets. The operation would kick off at a certain time and run on a server in a datacentre based on a predefined schedule.

Another model is to have robots regularly check a queue of tasks to be automated. The status can be indicated by a flag that tells the robot there is work to be done. The robot checks the flag and, if set, checks the source of new information, processes the information by connecting to the required system through its UI and then resets the flag. The source could be a spreadsheet containing new data.

The robot copies the data, then logs in to the relevant business system through its UI as if a human was signing into the system and pastes the new data into the appropriate fields. The data could be a packet of information, such as the name and details of a new customer registering an account on an online shop, or a new subscriber to a TV or newspaper service.

Having added the details of a new subscriber to the business system through its UI like a human would, then the robot goes back and checks the flag to see if there is more work to be done. The robots can put data in such queues that then activate other robots to take the process further, for example to activate another robot to add the customer details to a CRM system, and in turn activate a third robot to send a text of acknowledgement to the new subscriber. And so, bit by bit we can extend the level of business process automation in the organisation.

Figure 4.3 provides a graphical representation of the scenario described above.

Figure 4.3 An example of how unattended RPA can work

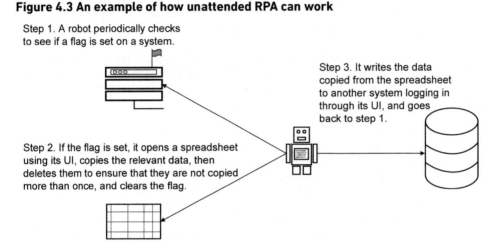

Step 1. A robot periodically checks to see if a flag is set on a system.

Step 3. It writes the data copied from the spreadsheet to another system logging in through its UI, and goes back to step 1.

Step 2. If the flag is set, it opens a spreadsheet using its UI, copies the relevant data, then deletes them to ensure that they are not copied more than once, and clears the flag.

This is known as unattended RPA and its devotees believe it is the only true way of automating tasks in order to take the robot out of the human.

Attended RPA This is when a human activates a robot, from their desktop, to run a certain task. It is also called RDA. Use case examples are prevalent in the contact centre. For example, an agent can activate a robot to update a field in a business application following a call from a customer providing new information or instructions to the company, such as a change of circumstance. The robot could also be activated by a chatbot that has collected the information from a customer either through text in chat messages or through conversational AI, talking to the customer.

The attended RPA robots integrate with other systems in very much the same way as unattended robots – they go through the UI. Some vendors interrogate the target applications and determine what type of connection is best suited to that application.

Some software vendors provide a capability to allow the robot developer to give the attended automation robot an avatar that resides on the user's desktop. The avatar acts as an assistant, and is activated when the tasks that it is programmed to do start. It pops up on-screen and asks if it can complete the task. The avatar can be given a voice interface powered by conversational AI.

I believe, over the next decade, this kind of development will evolve to deliver fully fledged personal IVAs to knowledge workers that are trained in the context of the work and consequently power the next productivity revolution.

Process orchestration

Processes are typically made up of different steps, often needing one step to be fully completed before the next one can be taken. There are also situations that could lead to a process continuing away from its main swim lane in order to satisfy certain conditions, for example, a simple change of address notification by a customer leading to a robot updating the address in several databases. However, if the robot could not easily confirm the identity of the customer, it might need to branch out from the main process flow to double-check the customer's ID and it might need to pass the task to a human to make a decision about the ID, who in turn passes the controls back to the robot. This is what is referred to as human-in-the-loop. The controls then have to be returned to the automated process for the task of address change to be completed. These require workflow, controls and orchestration capabilities.

In the past many companies made use of business process management (BPM) tools that offered features to manage the flow of control between machines and humans. Today we have to manage a more complex mix of robots to humans and to other systems. This is where intelligent BPM solutions and automation-specific orchestration tools have come to the fore. Many RPA solutions already offer workflow and orchestration capabilities within their own systems, but it is the management of controls across the end-to-end process where RPA and other types of process automation from multiple software vendors might be running that is needed. This has given rise to a new breed of third-party vendor software tools to help with the running of automated processes in the enterprise. These work across different automation tools and orchestrate the flow of controls and activation of robots.

Process and task mining

Process and task mining capture information from different sources of process data to virtually reconstruct how business is conducted in the enterprise and then analyse the information to make recommendations for optimising processes, mitigating risks and discovering opportunities for automating more processes. There are two main types of technologies to do this, process mining and task mining, with discovery offered by both. Some vendors offer one or the other and some provide both types of capabilities, either natively in their own platforms or in partnership with other vendors. It is worth asking vendors which or what combination of process and task mining their software solution offers when selecting software, what it takes to prepare for it, to deploy it, how long that is likely to take and what the costs would be.

Process mining
Enterprise software applications underpin many business processes and generate data about those processes in the form of application logs. These logs are great sources of information about how the processes are actually undertaken in the enterprise, for example if they are as standardised as the organisation believes them to be or, if not, what the variations are and what risks to the organisation these represent. I have heard tales of heads of operations almost breaking down when process mining reports have shown them 80 to 100 variations in what they thought to be a highly standardised process. The variations mean unknown risks and costs and the more of them there are, the higher the risks to the organisation.

In its traditional form, process mining software mines a major business application's logs to discover process steps and branches to virtually reconstruct how processes are undertaken when staff use the application. The process mining software analyses the data to work out where the bottlenecks are and what variations there are in standardised processes. Logs from more than one business application can be mined but you would have to create a data warehouse to bring all the data together for analysis purposes and that is likely to need significant investment in time and money as a project.

Process mining has been around longer than IA but it is going through something of a revival on the back of the success of RPA. This is because organisations, having automated the most obvious candidate processes for automation, want to know what to automate next. There are manual ways of doing this but process mining allows organisations to automate the finding of automation opportunities, and so process mining has become an important part of the IA spectrum of technologies.

Task mining
Another approach to getting process-related insights is to capture information from knowledge workers' computers. This is what I call task mining but it is also referred to as desktop mining. The approach uses code injection to capture task-related information or computer vision that analyses images of the users' screens. The kind of information that is collected includes what windows they open and what buttons they click. The software then reconstructs the processes based on this information.

The benefits of task mining include identification of bottlenecks or long-winded complex procedures that are not only a source of delays and costs to operations but real pain points for staff, which lead to frustration and job dissatisfaction. These can be identified and addressed. Having virtually reconstructed processes, best candidates for automation can also be identified based on factors such as volumes of transactions, the regularity of patterns of content flowing through the process and its complexity. Some solutions go further and automatically calculate and report the business case for automating the process based on its characteristics and known costs of implementing automation software.

Unsurprisingly, the concept of task mining can lead to fears of loss of privacy among staff. There are safeguards that can be put in place to address these issues. Measures include:

- ensuring that staff are on board with the project from the start and any data are collected with their permission;
- clear and well communicated objectives for the implementation and transparency on how the data will be used;
- proofs of concepts that show staff what to expect from the technology in practice;
- anonymisation of the data that are captured;
- allowing the staff to see what data are collected about them;
- creating a white list and a black list of applications that the task mining software can track on the user's desktop;
- clearly setting out the data privacy rules that are to be followed by the task mining software.

Once task mining is set up and the information is captured, AI is used to analyse it to join the dots to construct a visual representation of how processes are conducted in the target business area.

The AI in the solution improves deterministic statistical analysis, and supervised algorithms help with pattern matching.

An example of its application is a contact centre operator implementing the technology to find out how long its chat channel agents had to wait for messages to come in and what proportion of chats could be semi-automated based on the pattern and the complexity of the types of questions that customers posted on the channel.

To conclude this section, here is a summary of what insights process and task mining software can provide by capturing and analysing process information:

- identifying unnecessary steps and bottlenecks in workflows;
- discovering variations in processes and their likely impact on operations and business functions;
- optimising workload assignments and shift patterns;
- identifying candidate processes for automation based on factors such as:
  - frequency and volumes of transactions processed
  - demand for the process
  - costs of the operation as is and if the same is automated;
- automatically calculating the business case for automating candidate tasks, having discovered them through the mining;
- uncovering risks, for example where additional steps may be required in processes to improve resilience to system failures or to comply with regulatory requirements.

SUMMARY

In this chapter I described how AI can help many industries to run improved operations to achieve efficiency. I provided examples of better informed decision-making, improving the management of the supply chain, the use of AI to make farming more scientific to save on amounts of weed killer used, water for irrigation and optimal timing of planting, feeding and harvesting crops. I highlighted the use of AI in industrial plants to optimise power consumption. I then focused on business functions and knowledge work and provided an overview of IA for business process automation and the breadth of technologies that fall into this category, mostly powered by AI. These provide the quickest way for organisations to adopt AI for business efficiency. There are many off-the-shelf solutions in each of the IA constituent technologies that I have described. I have also provided examples of their use cases.

These pre-packaged technologies fall into the business function toolkits that I described in Chapter 2 and highlighted in Figure 2.1 'Classification of AI toolkits'. They help organisations to take steps towards becoming autonomous. AI is the major enabler of them and advanced digitalisation and process autonomics. We are still at the early stages of this journey but business pressures mean that we need to learn about the technologies to prepare for the journey.

To wrap up this chapter, Table 4.1 provides a few additional examples of use cases of IA in different functions and industries.

Table 4.1 More examples of use cases of IA in different functions and industries

Business function/ industry	Use case	How IA can help	Benefits	Challenges
Accounts payable	Many organisations receive invoices by the thousands and in a variety of different formats and layouts. These have to be checked for accuracy and compliance with corporate policies, and referenced against the relevant PO	An IDP solution extracts the required information from invoices, e.g. the quantities, amounts, PO number and cost centre. The data are then automatically checked against reference sources, then passed on for either approval using workflow or for settlement with the IDP directly interacting with the relevant systems or passing the information on to them using RPA. Anything that cannot be confirmed by the IDP solution is flagged as an exception and passed to a human for checking	• faster processing; • increased capacity; • reduced risks of errors; • systematic checking of invoices including checking for fraud; • increased business insight as data from operations can be captured quickly, e.g. at the point of invoice settlement rather than waiting for periodic financial reports; • similarly the accounting close process can be made easier with better financial insights; • performance data can be captured, e.g. if staff are too slow to deal with workflow-based approval processes	• ensuring the business case stacks up for small to medium-sized operations; • fully capturing all the process steps and variations to document for automation and for reference; • optimising processes for automated operations; • ensuring that the automations are maintained and updated when changes happen

(Continued)

Table 4.1 (Continued)

Business function/ industry	Use case	How IA can help	Benefits	Challenges
Central government	Ensuring faster benefits claim processing while mitigating risks of fraud	NLP and analytics can be used to check applicants' documents, extracting identity information then checking and verifying the data against reference sources AI can help contact centre staff to deal faster with applications and improve through processing as well as better communications with claimants ID checking and analysis can be augmented with social media information and other sources of data to mitigate risks of fraud, e.g. discover networks of criminal gangs fraudulently claiming benefits using fake identities	• automation speeds up claims application processing; • augmenting staff with AI provides them with information for faster processing of cases; • risks of fraud can be mitigated and costs reduced	• all of the above plus ensuring fair automated processing of claims. This requires testing with a representative dataset and checking of outcomes to feedback into continuous improvements
Loan servicing	Loan servicing is a document-intensive process. A lot of text has to be read, and key items of information such as the borrower's name and address, the outstanding amount of loan and interest rates identified, verified and processed	An IDP solution can be used to capture the required information and cross check and validate them against other documents and reference sources	• faster processing of loan servicing cases with automated reading of documents, information capture, referencing and validation; • improved quality of service with reduced data errors; • increased capacity to take on more work and grow revenues	• as above; • ensuring security of financial information; • ensuring that the end solution delivers in accordance with financial regulatory requirements

Table 4.1 (Continued)

Business function/industry	Use case	How IA can help	Benefits	Challenges
Healthcare	Settlement of healthcare invoices submitted by different medical workers and for use of hospital facilities to insurance companies can be extremely uncoordinated with delayed and poorly recorded submissions leading to confusion and error	A mix of IDP to read the invoices and capture key data, check for errors and potential fraud, followed by RPA to make the payment, update all the relevant systems and notify all stakeholders: practitioners, hospitals and patients	• data are updated across multiple systems and all parties are kept informed of the current status of payments for the treatment provided; • reduced rates of errors; • mitigating risks of fraudulent claims and increased revenue assurance	• as above

PART 2:
CASE STUDIES

In Part 2 I look at a number of case studies of real practical applications of AI in business and healthcare. The case studies show broad uses of AI in daily operations, ranging from customer contact management, to patient care and sales optimisation.

5   THE BIONIC CUSTOMER SERVICE AGENT AT SIEMENS GLOBAL BUSINESS SERVICES

In this case study I describe how Siemens Global Business Services (GBS) uses AI to enhance and augment its customer services. The company has used a variety of technologies to automate its processes, but the case study focuses on what the company refers to as the bionic agent. This is an intelligent solution that uses NLP and is being rolled out to automate the processing of seven million service tickets that Siemens GBS generates each year to track, action and manage its clients' enquiries. The solution was developed in-house using Microsoft Azure Services and is on course to automate 70 per cent of the work involved in handling the customer enquiries that come into the organisation. Its accuracy is already proven to be over 90 per cent, higher than when the work is done manually.

ABOUT SIEMENS GLOBAL BUSINESS SERVICES

Siemens GBS has more than 20 years' experience delivering shared business services to the Siemens group of companies. Today it provides smart and digital services to both internal and external customers. Its current portfolio comprises transactional and expertise-driven services. It employs around 10,000 staff and delivers services to its clients from 11 major delivery locations. These are highlighted in Figure 5.1.

The services that it offers include:

- Finance:
  - Opportunity-to-Cash services including lead generation, sales, order management, cash collection, accounts receivable and after sales services.
  - Purchase-to-Pay services from purchasing to accounts payable and payment execution and supply chain services.
  - Record-to-Report services from finance records to closing reports.
- HR:
  - Hire-to-Retire services from recruiting to retirement.
  - Temporary personnel including contracting and payroll services.
  - Contingent labour administration and management.
  - Lifelong development and learning.

- Business solutions and services that are expertise driven and project-based including technical translation services, communications and logistics services.
  - The logistics business includes delivery management.
- Engineering services to provide technology-based solution design and software engineering.
- Project transformation and consultancy services to provide customers with functional process expertise and deliver operational support out of a project management pool.

Figure 5.1 The global service network of Siemens GBS

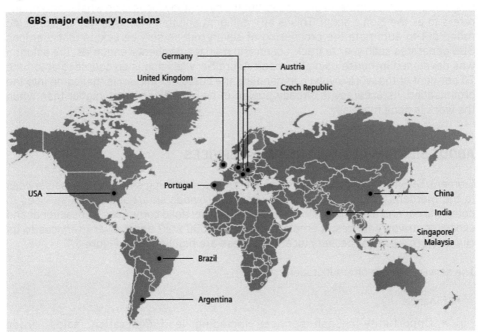

GBS major delivery locations

THE BUSINESS CONTEXT

As an organisation that started as a shared services centre, efficiency has always been important for Siemens GBS. The means of achieving it have traditionally included labour arbitrage, centralisation of services, specialisation and scale that lead to savings through synergies, sharing of resources and standardisation. Today, there is increased focus on technology as an enabler of efficiency and innovation to drive business outcomes faster whilst maintaining the benefits of the shared services model. To this end, Siemens GBS is increasingly taking advantage of technology. Each year, it runs programmes for service modernisation to improve capacity and straight through processing. The company sees this as a necessity to stay ahead in a world where disruption can happen very quickly. New players can emerge with novel business models powered by technology that quickly capture a share of the market, leaving established corporations in a tailspin as they struggle to modernise legacy systems and service models that are difficult to change.

One of the fields of technology that Siemens GBS has invested in is IA to improve process and service efficiency. In 2019, it took part in *Enterprise Intelligent Automation Adoption Maturity | Pinnacle Model Analysis*, a study by Everest Group (Everest Group, 2020) to identify large companies that had developed best-in-class IA capabilities and were achieving the best outcomes. Everest Group assessed 49 enterprises including Siemens GBS that, after extensive assessment, was judged to be the leader in the group.

Siemens GBS started implementing IA technologies in 2017 and by 2019 it had automated over 450 processes. Examples included an intelligent inventory recommender that used machine learning and predictive analytics combined with RPA to optimise stock levels and subsequently reduce the total inventory value for its clients by more than 30 per cent. It also provided automation of logistics for parts. Other examples include its use of IoT combined with data analytics and RPA to enable predictive machine maintenance, automated invoice processing and IT incident management where RPA robots capture incident information from different systems and create tickets in the service management software.

THE BIONIC AGENT FOR SERVICE TICKET PROCESSING

The scale of Siemens GBS' operations around the globe has resulted in the company having to deal with millions of service tickets generated each year. The service tickets are created following every customer enquiry, be it by phone, email or via other interaction channels. These add up to more than seven million tickets each year. The enquiries come in mostly by email despite Siemens GBS having implemented self-service portals where its clients can access service information and see the status of work in progress. Additionally, it has deployed chatbots provided on the self-service portals to answer customer enquiries. The figure of seven million tickets a year excludes the customer interactions that have been completed by the chatbots.

Another channel operated by Siemens GBS is email provided with function-specific mailboxes, for example for specific finance or HR services. The majority of all enquiries come in through this channel. Contact by phone is also supported. To keep track of interactions and their status and management, every customer contact that is made via the phone is logged in the ticketing system manually by staff.

The bionic agent was developed to automate the process of handling these enquiries; to make the customer services faster and more efficient. How it was developed is described in the next section.

The emails describing the nature of the enquiries have to be read, the context understood and appropriate action taken or planned. These can be simple questions, for example a client asking what the status of a PO is, or they can be more complex, such as an email informing the organisation that a whole chain of approvals is to be updated as a result of personnel changes. Sometimes they come in with documents attached, the content of which have to be read, understood and taken into account when handling the enquiry.

Under the hood of the bionic agent

The bionic agent uses NLP to handle the incoming unstructured data, that is the text in the emails. The bionic agent does what a human would do; it reads and classifies the information in the text. It then interprets the data and, in response, activates the relevant workflow. It was developed in stages in-house, initially in the Purchase-to-Pay (P2P) function to simply identify the exact nature of the incoming request and to send it to the right group of staff for processing. Siemens GBS has extended the software functionality over time to do more.

It uses a number of algorithms as follows.

Classification
Powered by text mining, the first algorithm indexes and classifies the enquiry based on its content. Through extensive training of the model with historical data, Siemens GBS reports that it has achieved over 90 per cent accuracy in the classification capability. According to the company, the algorithm has made the decision-making more objective than when humans do it. This is because of the machine's ability to rapidly relate the information to a huge volume of historical data, to compare the context and classify the incoming customer enquiry. The Siemens GBS team believe this aspect clearly demonstrates how AI can augment human activity. Some of their human service centre agents have learnt from the decisions that the machine has made, and consequently become more objective in their decision-making.

Prioritisation
After the classification, another algorithm prioritises the tickets. This is based on the nature of the enquiry and the estimated urgency. To do this, sentiment analysis is also undertaken to work out the urgency as perceived by the client based on the language used in the email or other interactions. Each ticket is then prioritised and gets assigned a response time within service level agreements (SLAs).

Entity extraction
The third machine learning model is used to extract entities that decide what action is to be taken in response, for example in a procurement context, identifying the PO number or if the approvals need changing, extracting who was the original approver and who is the new one. Other activities include data validation using predefined taxonomies and rules.

After the entity extraction the appropriate workflow is activated, and all the relevant information is passed to the automated solution that services that workflow. This can be an RPA robot that takes the information and updates the field in the relevant business system, for example changing the name of the approver in the purchasing system. Or it can be a direct data update to a business system using RESTful application programming interfaces (REST APIs).

In this way, using NLP, unstructured information is converted to structured data that can be automatically put into the relevant business system. That data update might complete the activity that was needed in response to the ticket being generated or it might activate another chain of processes, many of which are automated too, for example an update sent to a supplier.

Completion

The final step is to go back to the client who raised the service request with a response. This too is partially automated with the information being provided to a human agent to be checked before a reply is sent to the client. Siemens GBS made the decision to have humans handle this final customer interaction. It refers to it as its quality gate where humans check the work that has been done by the machine and then reply to the client.

The solution development

Siemens GBS has a large technology group as well as an innovation team that comes up with ideas for new solutions to enhance the company's services. The group can also respond to demand from the business to deal with their specific requirements. In this case, the service ticket handling was a very high-volume process that took a lot of manual effort. Consequently, the team assigned to the project scanned the market for out-of-the-box technologies that were available at the time, but they needed to develop a capability that offered them reusability. They also wanted a cloud-based and highly scalable solution. As a result, they selected Microsoft Azure Services. They have been working in partnership with Microsoft on the development of the solution.

In addition, in terms of skills, the team could draw upon AI skills within the corporate technology group as well as their teams in Portugal and Czechia.

Having set up the project and created the development team, it took nine months to build the minimum viable bionic agent. Initially, it just classified the information captured from the service tickets and routed them to the right teams for action. They ran a proof of concept for six weeks and saw that they could unlock higher value work by speeding up ticket processing times and freeing up staff from having to do that initial task. They then added the entity extraction and then the rest. They had to ensure that the bionic agent was secure and that it complied with corporate digital and HR policies, International Organization for Standardization information security standards. and regulations such as the General Data Protection Regulation. There was a lot of learning through trial and error to get the right algorithm and to increase its accuracy.

The core engine is NLP, and the design is such that it allows the bionic agent to be applied to other requirements. In future it might be trained to extract other entities and be applied to other use cases in the company.

The benefits

Siemens GBS has generated significant benefits from the bionic agent already. Where it is deployed, service ticket resolution effort has been 70 per cent automated with roll-out to more areas of business planned.

The bionic agent has enabled its staff to work on higher value processes such as complex cases that cannot be automated or analysis of customer contact data to improve services. Additionally, the company has built the foundations for an intelligent solution that can be adapted and reused to speed up and enhance other services. This work is ongoing, and we expect to see more efficiencies generated by Siemens GBS in the near future.

The company has also increased its AI skills and will be able to develop new products in its pursuit of new technology solutions to innovate and stay ahead of competition.

SUMMARY

In this chapter we learnt how Siemens GBS developed its bionic customer service agent to speed up the processing of service tickets that are generated in response to customer queries each year. The bionic agent is based on NLP and automates 70 per cent of the ticket handling processes. The rest is completed by staff who check the work that has been done before completing the task associated with each ticket by responding to the customer.

The bionic agent was developed in-house based on Microsoft Azure Services, with the ability to deploy on cloud for scalability.

This case study shows us how organisations can turn large parts of their business processes into autonomous operations while still having people involved, not only to develop the solutions, but also to manage and monitor the automated processes, to handle more complex tasks, as well as to deal with direct customer interactions. This is exactly how I believe most knowledge work in the enterprise will be delivered in the future. This is an evolution rather than a revolution because it will happen by degrees as intelligent technologies are enhanced and improved.

There are several other important lessons to learn from Siemens GBS' bionic agent:

- That it can augment the work of the human agents, for example help them to become more objective in process-related decision-making.
- AI can be combined with other technologies to scale up process automation and consequently the benefits that can be derived from it, for example AI with RPA leading to 70 per cent of service ticket processing being automated.
- That AI-based solutions can be developed with reusability in mind. They can be repurposed to operate in different business contexts, for example even in one function area that can handle PO as well as invoice enquiries.
- That if you cannot find the solution that you need in a business function toolkit, you can develop your own with much of the infrastructure needed provided by AI platform vendors.

Finally, Siemens GBS is not intimidated by the complexity of smart technology. Its approach is all about trialling things with a proof of concept, building a skills base, learning by doing and building on successes. This is an approach that I cannot recommend more.

6 RETAINING THE HUMAN TOUCH AT CALDERDALE COUNCIL

In this case study I look at the use of an IVA at Calderdale Council in England. In my view this case study exemplifies application of best practice. It shows how a joined-up, inclusive approach supported by executives and with good stakeholder communication can deliver great success. Another important aspect of this case study is that it showcases how intelligent solutions can be enhanced post-deployment to respond to changing conditions and requirements. Finally, it demonstrates that the solutions can be simple and updated by non-technical staff.

BACKGROUND

Local government organisations around the world are under constant pressure to provide services to satisfy increasing demand while their budgets are cut. Calderdale Council is no exception, and consequently, it has had to undertake major programmes of work to reduce the cost of services while at the same time improving the customer experience. The style of interactions with citizens is also changing with demand for digital channels going up.

In 2018, the council started to implement an IVA. It had already refreshed its website and introduced intelligent forms. It had also operated a live chat channel that was first introduced in 2014. The IVA was to advance its digitalisation and omnichannel support objectives. Given that the council serves customers with varied needs, it was essential for it to continue to provide an option for citizens to interact with human advisors for open and empathetic conversations. Ensuring that the option to chat with a person is always available is one reason the automated channel has been successful. Customers have been free to choose rather than feeling constrained by the automation.

In 2014, 70 per cent of customer contacts were over the phone. By March 2020 that figure had fallen to 30 per cent. Over the same period customer satisfaction also improved. Careful implementation, led from the top, with a keen eye on the business benefits and the human angle have produced these impressive results.

ABOUT CALDERDALE COUNCIL

Calderdale Council serves approximately 210,000 citizens in Yorkshire, England. It is a metropolitan borough council so it provides a wide range of local services from libraries and leisure centres to road maintenance and waste services. It employs 2,600 people and has a vision for 2024 to transform the major towns in the borough. Figure 6.1 shows the geographic area covered by the council.

Figure 6.1 Geographic area covered by Calderdale Council

THE BUSINESS CONTEXT

Local government organisations in England have been under intense budgetary pressure. From 2011 to 2018 central government funding to all local authorities was reduced by 49 per cent (National Audit Office, 2019) in real terms against a backdrop of increasing demand for services due to the aging population.

Other organisations can adopt radical policies to reduce the level of service to meet cost constraints but social and legislative pressure mean that is not an option for local government. The only option is to carefully balance reducing costs with the need to ensure that statutory duties and the needs of society are still met. In technology terms, this means increasing automation of business processes for efficiency while ensuring that there is no barrier to the empathetic human contact that many citizens need when they contact their local authority.

The council responded with a programme of improvement covering all aspects of customer access. Digital by choice became its benchmark for service provision with chat a major channel for online engagement and improving the customer experience. These requirements drove the introduction of the virtual assistant for handling short transactional interactions, while keeping access to contact centre agents open to continue to provide empathetic services with the human touch.

INTRODUCING VIRA

Having successfully deployed live chat in 2014, the council decided to take the next step to introduce an IVA to support self-service and provide consistently high-quality experiences to customers who contacted the council outside normal working hours. The IVA was to help website visitors by signposting them to online forms and the My Account customer portal.

A project team was set up in November 2018 staffed with the contact centre team leader and advisors, plus staff from the council's IT and web teams. They also engaged an external partner to provide development and related professional services. The IVA that Calderdale Council developed is called VIRA (Virtual, Interactive, Responsive Assistant) and it has been trained and implemented to respond to questions in certain categories.

There are a few points to mention about VIRA. First of all, the customer has the option to chat with an advisor at any time. The council considers it very important that their customers use the virtual assistant because it is convenient but that they never feel stuck in an automated channel. Secondly, the whole customer access strategy fits together, meaning that web chat was implemented to help keep customers on a self-service channel. This also means that the council can get insights to understand when customers break off from that channel and choose to use the phone or visit the council in person. These jump-off points can be traced and fixed.

Alongside website improvements there was a significant effort put into improving the large number of web forms needed on the site and ensuring that the high-volume forms were part of an end-to-end process both within the council and from the customer's perspective.

The implementation

The first implementation was a pilot to help with council tax enquiries that came in via its human-operated chat channel. The business area was chosen because it had the most demand across all channels per year. Popular customer queries and outcomes provided by the agents were identified and categorised for training purposes, to guide customers to fill in an online form, refer them back to the office and email a response or complete the enquiry during the chat. Additionally, the project team had to pre-emptively think of all the likely questions that customers might ask VIRA and the variations in the words that they might use.

The first version of VIRA was released to a community of users. These were still internal to the council and its associated agencies and not the public. VIRA went through six to seven weeks of testing in the community. The testing demonstrated that it could handle the type of vocabulary that was used by real people in real circumstances. A lot of the set-up of VIRA and its training had been informed by previous chat histories, that is, words and sentence constructs that people had used prior to VIRA when the chat channel was operated by the contact centre personnel.

While the initial parts of the configuration set-up and training were undertaken by the council's service partner working in collaboration with the most experienced contact centre agents, post-implementation staff were trained to add new words and intents to its vocabulary. This continues today and allows staff in the contact centre to train VIRA to handle new areas of business as well as respond to changing requirements. The changes are easy to make without any technical input and no coding is required. VIRA is also available on smartphones and tablets as well as Calderdale Council's website. While vocabulary updates can be made as simply as editing text, each change requires testing before taking the enhanced VIRA into production. The changes typically take half a day to implement.

When the COVID-19 pandemic hit the country the contact centre advisors had to respond very quickly to changes in both policies and structures. This ability to update VIRA's capabilities fast to handle new types of enquiries from citizens has been a great advantage.

During the implementation, the council developed a short customer survey to be offered on every chat to gauge customer reaction and satisfaction with the channel. During the pilot, the team sent out a new weekly newsletter to all customer services advisors and other stakeholders to keep them abreast of VIRA's development and implementation and the potential benefits that it would bring to their part of the service.

VIRA typically connects the customer to a web resource, to information or a web form for example. The majority of questions are answered satisfactorily in this way. The council has built safeguards into the process; certain topics, such as bereavement or disability, automatically connect the customer to a human advisor.

The service went live in March 2019. It is worth emphasising that the option to connect to an advisor is available at any time so the customer does not feel that they are being pushed into using the automated channel.

Scaling up VIRA

With these foundations in place, and having gone into production for council tax chat services, further work could then proceed on enhancing VIRA to take in more service areas. Council tax was soon joined by waste services. At this point the world changed as the COVID-19 hit in early 2020 and that meant the council having to make reactive changes to policies and procedures quickly, often with a need to implement the changes overnight. As mentioned previously, VIRA could be rapidly updated by staff in the customer contact operation with no need to refer to technical departments for these updates; they could be approved, tested and released in a matter of hours. By this stage in the development of VIRA, customers were getting around 70 per cent of their queries satisfied directly with about 30 per cent of the sessions being referred to an advisor.

To progress further, the implementation team felt that some of the interactions could benefit by being made more conversational. Subsequently, after some discussion and assessments of requirements, the underlying product was changed to the Oracle Digital Assistant. Furthermore, the team increased their focus in several areas:

- Determining the best path for an individual customer to take by using the information in their questions and consequently directing them to the answers in the right context. For example the question 'What is my balance?' can be interpreted several different ways. The context has to be taken into account before the customer starts the dialogue to determine their council tax balance when they might have meant the balance on their rent account.

- A more conversational path to be taken when needed to resolve ambiguity by asking the customer further questions and then directing them to the right resources.

- With social media becoming ever more popular, the council was keen to provide support for a wide variety of channels starting with their own website, Facebook Messenger and text/SMS.

The upshot was a renewed version of VIRA with the ability to answer more questions in the target subject areas.

Initially, frequent team meetings were held to review VIRA's interactions and responses to enhance its performance. Today, meetings are held on an ad hoc basis when additional support is needed. These are typically to do with language and recognition of intents.

A set of dashboards has been implemented to allow the team to monitor intents. These show answers matched to intents and those escalated to an agent, and most popular expressions. The latter dashboard highlights expressions that VIRA had issues with and provides further drill down analysis to help with enhancing its performance.

Under the hood of the solution

VIRA uses NLP to interpret what the customer is saying. Initially it was based on Oracle Virtual Assistant and then was moved to Oracle Digital Assistant, which allowed more flexibility in the way conversations were handled. Figures 6.2 and 6.3 show the solution overview and a high-level view of typical customer journeys.

Figure 6.2 The solution overview

Public website	Oracle Digital Assistant	Oracle Service Cloud
	Immediate answers to questions	Web chat
	Dialogues to guide customers when needed	Video chat

Comprehensive information pages about citizen services and approximately 160 web forms.	The digital assistant, VIRA, answers approximately 70% of the questions in the subject areas it serves.	The remaining 30% of enquiries are routed to an advisor. The advisor uses a web chat workbench and in future will be able to switch to video chat if preferred.

The solution development

I particularly like the approach that Calderdale Council took to develop the solution. It is a great example of best practice that led to the council's success. Firstly, a strong internal team was mobilised with good executive support. Secondly, responsibility was devolved to the team of people that had to operate the end-solution; that is, the contact centre team. This was very important given that they were the team that after the implementation would have to carry out changes to the NLP in VIRA to ensure that it could deal well with words, terms and language usage as a whole.

Thirdly, the council also ensured that all stakeholders were kept informed of developments and progress. They instigated a customer survey to understand how customers were finding the service and their satisfaction levels.

Fourthly, there was a complete feedback loop that was used to gather performance and satisfaction data to feed back into enhancements to VIRA and the service as a whole. Furthermore, VIRA was very much a part of the bigger picture digitalisation of council services to make it possible to provide excellent self-service experiences for citizens.

There was a good partnership with the council's service providers and suppliers as well. The dynamics worked well powered by good communication – another important part of best practice.

Figure 6.3 Customer journeys guided by VIRA

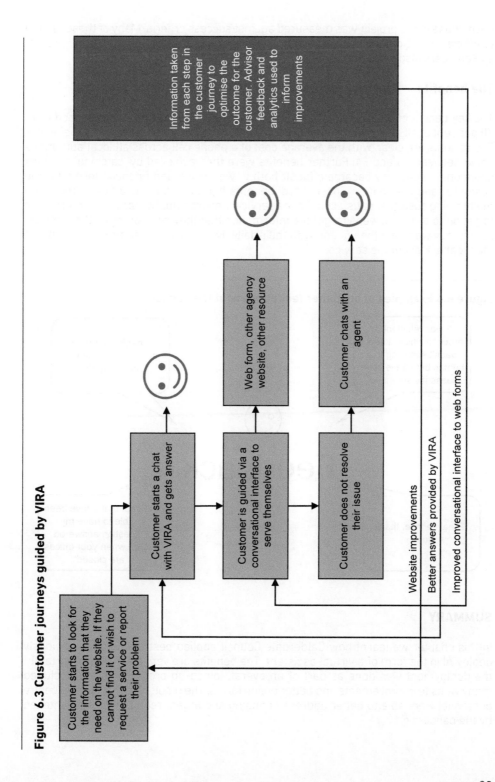

Each phase of the project was measured against success criteria. Many of these related to efficiency but customer satisfaction was measured at each stage and the internal stakeholders also carefully managed.

The benefits

The key benefit of the overall programme is that telephone contact was reduced from 70 per cent of all customer contact to 30 per cent with improved customer satisfaction. The benefits are clear, with the average cost of a phone call across all local authorities being between £3 and £4. Further benefits were then achieved by 'catching' complex situations before they became difficult both in well-being and financial terms for the customer and the council. These 'hard' benefits had to be balanced at all times with maintaining customer satisfaction in the service. Unsurprisingly, many customers want to get on to a council website, get the information that they need or make the request/ report they want and then get on with their daily lives. Figure 6.4 summarises some of the feedback about the service.

Figure 6.4 Examples of customer feedback about the service

"I was reluctant to proceed when I knew I wasn't speaking to a human but I have been pleasantly surprised".

"Thank you for the advice, I will use this service again".

Feedback

"Great service, thank you".

"Great that I have been able to have my question answered even when your offices are closed".

SUMMARY

In this chapter we learnt how Calderdale Council applied best practice to judiciously deploy AI in the form of a virtual assistant. The benefits are very clear but, importantly, the deployment was done as part of an overall joined-up programme that included many website improvements and better online forms. The result was that contact centre personnel were able to better address changing and urgent requirements heightened by the pandemic.

The development took place in incremental steps, each of which was measured against success criteria. Although one of the prime objectives was efficiency, other criteria included customer and employee satisfaction.

Informed by feedback from customers and the analytics, incremental improvements have been implemented to get better answers and cover more complex queries. The council is intending to maintain this continuous improvement cycle and yield more benefits.

7   AI IMPROVING STROKE CARE AT THE ROYAL BERKSHIRE NHS FOUNDATION TRUST

You don't have to be an AI scientist to enjoy reading about new AI developments that are good for mankind and the planet. An excellent example is the use of AI at the Royal Berkshire NHS Foundation Trust (RBFT) in Reading, England, to examine CT scan images of brains of stroke patients to identify the extent of damage and to highlight early changes that might not be visible to the physician. The software is not a diagnostic tool but helps doctors to decide the best care pathways for stroke patients, as well as speeding up their treatment. It addresses one of the main obstacles to faster treatment of stroke patients, and that is the possible lack of neuroradiology imaging expertise on site when patients present out of hours. By augmenting the general physicians' decisions and accelerating treatment along the appropriate stroke pathway, the risks of patients suffering permanent brain damage or death are minimised.

It has been used at RBFT since March 2020 and it has already helped to improve care as part of a series of measures that include increased collaborative working with a network of hospitals in the Thames Valley in England. The AI software has boosted the ability of the network to share scan images on hand-held devices and smartphones to allow emergency non-specialist doctors to connect with specialists out of hours. The combination of these factors means that care compared with before the deployment has improved:

- Door-in-door-out time, the time that it takes to get a patient diagnosed and sent to a specialist hospital, has almost halved from 140 minutes to 79 minutes.
- Referral time has shrunk by 75 per cent from 77 minutes to 44.
- Most importantly, patient outcomes have seen a significant improvement with initial data indicating a tripling of the rate of those who achieve independence after a major stroke.

ABOUT RBFT

The RBFT is one of the largest NHS trusts in England. It has multiple sites across Berkshire, the largest of which is Royal Berkshire Hospital in Reading. It provides specialist services such as cancer, dialysis and eye surgery to a wider population across Berkshire and beyond its borders. Where stroke care is concerned it has joined forces with other trusts to create a regional stroke collaboration partnership that is known as the Thrombectomy Innovation and Transformation Network (TITAN). The other hospitals in the partnership are located in Aylesbury, High Wycombe, Milton Keynes, Northampton, Oxford and Swindon.

RBFT has a 'digital by default' vision to extend its use of digital technologies to improve health outcomes.

THE HEALTHCARE CONTEXT

Stroke is a devastating condition that, according to the Stroke Association (Stroke Association, n.d.), strikes every five minutes in the UK, affecting 100,000 people each year. It can happen anywhere, often in the patient's local community where specialist stroke care might be out of reach. Time is of the essence to save a person from disabling long-term effects or even death.

Treatment involves intravenous thrombolysis (IVT) but in the case of large vessel strokes, patients are likely to need mechanical thrombectomy (MT) as well to remove any resulting blood clots. This is a specialist treatment that only some hospitals are able to perform.

Availability of specialists such as radiologists with the right skills at the time of treatment can also make a big difference to the outcome. Accordingly, there are two care pathways for stroke patients highlighted in Figure 7.1 (Nagaratnam, 2020).

In Figure 7.1, in the mothership model, the patient is taken direct to the specialist hospital where full stroke treatment can be offered including both IVT and MT. In the other pathway, the drip and ship model, the patient is taken to the nearest hospital and a computerised tomography angiography (CT/CTA) scan of their head is taken to assess the type of stroke and to administer IVT. Patients diagnosed with large blood clots who will need MT have to be transferred to a specialist unit as quickly as possible. Roughly two million neurons die in the brain every minute as a result of large blood clots starving them of oxygen.

Figure 7.1 The stroke thrombectomy pathway (Source: Nagaratnam, 2020)

Diagnosis of a large vessel occlusion (LVO) using CTA images requires skills and experience. During normal working hours, radiologists and stroke specialists can work collaboratively to assess the extent of the damage caused by the stroke shown in the CT/CTA scans. The need for accurate and speedy diagnosis remains and is particularly acute when an emergency happens out of hours. This is when the emergency department doctor or non-specialist doctor needs to reach the right specialists to consult them and that may take some time. There is also the speed of transferring medical images electronically to the specialists' laptops, if they are working remotely because of their shift patterns. In some cases this can take 20 minutes or more but in the case of stroke treatment, every minute matters. The speedier the treatment the more likely a patient will recover and return to normal life.

The e-Stroke suite

As part of its stroke care enhancements, RBFT had already joined others in the TITAN partnership to streamline the drip and ship model. As well as optimising some of the manual steps taken in patient care along this pathway, in 2019–20 it started to examine the possibility of using AI to help doctors diagnose CT/CTA scans. The aim of adding AI to the care pathway was to speed up diagnosis for those needing essential MT.

In March 2020, RBFT started to trial the use of AI. They implemented e-Stroke Suite developed by Oxford-based Brainomix Ltd. This is a set of intelligent tools for non-contrast CT and CTA brain scans. It is a decision-support tool that helps doctors to assess the damage caused by stroke. Since its deployment, it has been used in scans of more than 1,200 patients at RBFT to date, and physicians believe that it provides very high accuracy for proximal vessel occlusion in the anterior circulation type of LVO – that is, blood clots in front of the brain. It is not designed to detect other abnormalities such as tumours – it has to be used in the right context.

Close collaboration with all stakeholders from the outset was essential. These included the stroke specialists and the emergency department, the radiologists, the hospital IT departments, the teams in charge of treatment and information governance and the supplier.

In 2020, the implementation of the cloud version of e-Stroke was fast tracked because of the COVID-19 pandemic, which resulted in stretched hospital resources and unavailability of specialists due to self-isolation. This allowed images to be made available on smartphones at high speed so that specialists could see them no matter where they were, travelling to and from the hospital or isolating at home due to coming into contact with COVID-19.

While RBFT pioneered the use of the e-Stroke system in Reading, and rolled it out in March 2020, five other partner hospitals in the Thames Valley followed suit in June 2020. These were:

- Milton Keynes University Hospital;
- Wycombe General Hospital;
- Great Western Hospital;

- Northampton General Hospital;
- John Radcliffe Hospital (JRH), Oxford.

JRH in Oxford is one of the neuroscience specialist centres that provides thrombectomy services to the other hospitals in the Thames Valley area. The implementation of e-Stroke servers at all these hospitals allows them to share CT scanned images quickly for patients that are being referred. The sharing of images is done within data privacy regulations.

UNDER THE HOOD OF THE TECHNOLOGY

The Brainomix technology is based on neural networks and deep learning. It is trained like a doctor to analyse images to spot signs of cerebral bleeding and serious or irreversible damage. The company uses images and data from around the world to train its algorithms.

It can identify ischaemic changes to the brain (caused by the lack of blood and oxygen) as well as LVO and collateral vessel density in the anterior circulation, front of the brain. It uses a heatmap to show the regions of the brain that have been affected, and within each region to the pixel, whether it has detected any damage. In other words, e-Stroke assesses the patient for cerebral bleeding. It then shows the doctor any irreversible brain damage and LVO. It measures and highlights the damage and at-risk tissue.

e-Stroke can also handle multiphase CTA to detect the core – that is where the most damage is caused by the stroke – and the effect on collateral blood flow around the core. It creates a composite image from the different phases of the multiphase CTA to show the blood flow, highlighting where the blockages are, as shown in Figure 7.2. Consequently, it can provide temporal information to reveal slower collateral blood flow.

The benefits

e-Stroke was a major contributor to better diagnosis of brain issues in stroke patients at RBFT. In addition to the speeding up of door-in-door-out and referral times mentioned at the beginning of this chapter, improvements include:

- Patient outcomes, which has seen a significant improvement with initial data indicating a tripling of the rate of those who achieve independence after a major stroke.
- Faster communication and sharing of CT/CTA scan images with other medical teams in the TITAN group including the ability to view images on hand-held devices and smartphones. This means that during the pandemic, the hospital has been able to maintain the acute care pathway while many consultants were working remotely.
- While working remotely, the implementation of e-Stroke at RBFT meant that the consultants/specialists were not only able to diagnose the impact of stroke on patients, they could also take over the care of patients to free up emergency department doctors to get on with other cases.

Figure 7.2 An example of stroke damage image analysis provided by e-Stroke

Challenges

There was some scepticism amongst the clinicians about the reliability and the role of AI initially. However, the successful application of the technology in other European centres and the Trust's 'digital by default' vision and objective have helped with adoption of the technology at RBFT. Further trials at RBFT confirmed the effectiveness of the software as a decision-support tool for LVO. However, because of the pandemic, resources were not available to make extensive comparisons with other products on the market. The adoption of e-Stroke Cloud was fast tracked to maintain the care pathway during the COVID-19 pandemic.

After the deployment it became clear that manual upload of images from the scanner to the e-Stroke server could take longer than expected – up to 30 minutes. Something had to be done to reduce the time that it took. Subsequently the implementation team automated the upload. The images are today fed automatically from the scanner to e-Stroke and the upload time has reduced significantly. Analysis of data from December 2020 to January 2021 of 85 head scans (Nagaratnam, 2020) conducted manually show:

- 85 CT head scans:
  - average scan to upload time – 34 minutes (range 17 seconds–40 minutes);
  - average processing time – 1 minute 25 seconds;
- 42 CT carotid angiograms:
  - average scan to upload time – 23 minutes (range 3–40 minutes);
  - average processing time – 2 minutes.

Analysis of data collected from May to June 2021 after automation of the image upload process:

- 99 CT head scans:
  - average scan to upload time – 7 minutes (range 2–28 minutes);
  - average processing time – 1 minute 26 seconds;
- 59 CT carotid angiograms:
  - average scan to upload time – 8 minutes (range 5–14 minutes);
  - average processing time – 1 minute 21 seconds.

Another challenge is maintaining the AI and ensuring that as new advances and developments in the field of medicine happen, the AI is kept up to date too, that it can work with advances in imaging and diagnosis techniques. This is something that the clinical champion at RBFT is aiming to address over time.

Outlook for the future

This case study has highlighted the use of AI for a particular type of stroke in the front of the brain (anterior circulation). Roughly 20 per cent of patients present with strokes that affect the back of the brain (posterior circulation). Given the success of the current system, we are likely to see demand grow for intelligent decision-support systems for those other types of patients too, leading to future products that can handle more types of strokes.

We are also likely to see requirements for software vendors to show equality and fairness in their AI training; for example, show that the training was done using a sample that included people of all ages, and not limited to certain age groups or ethnicity. This should improve outcomes for all patients.

There is likely to be more standardised governance for introducing AI into healthcare as well. While there are clear procedures for introducing new drugs, governance for implementing new AI tools is currently ambiguous. There's a need for standardised guidelines on assessing competing solutions and checking their efficacy and safety before introducing them.

SUMMARY

This case study provides a great example of the use of AI for good – to enhance clinical outcomes for stroke patients. It shows that doubt and reluctance to embrace new technology can be overcome, and that lengthy procurement processes can be accelerated at times of emergency to ensure the quality of care. The thing that I like about it the most is that the deployment was led by clinicians, domain experts. These specialists wanted to ensure access to good stroke care at any time and anywhere, no matter where and when the patient presented. They are not resting on their laurels either and despite facing tough challenges in the pandemic, they are looking to see how else they could use AI to improve their processes to realise more benefits for patients.

8   AI IN SALES OPTIMISATION AT WÄRTSILÄ

Symbolic AI or Good Old Fashioned AI has been around for decades and continues to deliver business value. In this case study I showcase its use in conjunction with constraints inference (see the Glossary at the front of this book for a definition) in a configure price quote (CPQ) system at Wärtsilä where it is used to optimise and partially automate the complicated process of selling engines and other marine and energy products. Some of the company's products, such as generator engines or ship engines, are huge and are made up of many parts and components. It takes time, effort and expertise to agree all the details with a client in order to produce a quote.

To speed up this process and to reduce lead times, Wärtsilä implemented an intelligent CPQ solution that uses symbolic AI techniques to first capture knowledge from experts and then use it to guide the specialist sales consultants through the product specification process as they talk the customer through the available options and refine the product configuration. At the end of the process a bill of materials (BoM) is produced from which the product can be priced and a quote prepared.

The introduction of AI in the sales process has significantly reduced the time that it takes to produce quotes for customers, cutting the process time from days to a matter of hours. It has improved the quality of the quotes as they are based on real-time data about components and parts. It has also helped to optimise the sales cycle by efficiently producing the BoM that is then passed on to the engineering teams for product specification and production. Furthermore, it has reduced the time that technical sales consultants spend on preparing quotes, making them available to handle more customer interactions.

ABOUT WÄRTSILÄ

Headquartered in Helsinki, Finland, Wärtsilä is an international supplier of products, solutions and services to the marine and energy sectors with approximately 18,000 employees worldwide. In 2020, Wärtsilä had revenues of €4.6 billion. It operates in over 200 locations in 80 countries.

The company has been using AI for different business needs for many years. In this case study we focus on the sales optimisation application.

THE BUSINESS CONTEXT

When you buy a new car you are given many options, such as the type of engine, wheels, the material for the seat covers and other trim inside the car. These are complicated enough but you get even more options when buying an engine for a ship or to generate power, for example there will be options for the power rating, fuel type, emissions and maximum speed of the engine. There may be options for the position of the turbocharger and the layout of the exhaust pipes. There may be different types of pumps available and alternatives for air filtration and so on.

These options are linked, for example the position of the turbocharger could exclude some of the options for the size and the layout of the connecting pipes. You could do the configuration manually to create a BoM with hundreds of lines of items and each one in turn made up of smaller parts and components. The process would be lengthy and prone to human error.

THE SALES OPTIMISATION SOLUTION

The configurator is based on an intelligent solution that has a low-code platform for automation of knowledge capture and decision-making. Combined with a database of product information, it captures configuration decisions made by human experts to build the rules and make the constraints trees – tables of valid feature combinations – that it then uses to automate the configuration process for sales optimisation, described above. The trees guide the technical sales consultant through the available options. At each step, the software provides a menu of options, and narrows down the list as the customer makes their choices. The more features of the engine that are decided, the more the choices reduce until the customer gets a configuration that is tailored to their requirements. The output of the process is the BoM that is fed into the quoting system that then generates a quote. The BoM is used to create the product specification that the engineers will use to build the engine as well. It is also used for stock control and ordering the required components. The configurator is also available online as a self-service option for the client.

At Wärtsilä, they have been using AI for sales optimisation for well over a decade. Initially they used a consulting firm to develop the solution but, as time went by, they developed skills internally and today develop most of the enhancements and any additional requirements in-house. The sales optimisation software is used widely in the division and it is maintained by a team of about 10 technical personnel. The updating with new product information – the knowledge capture – is done in collaboration with subject matter experts. This is ongoing work given that Wärtsilä develops new products, and that components from third parties also change. The solution database of information and the knowledge associated with them has to be updated accordingly. This is all done in-house.

The benefits

In addition to the benefits that have already been highlighted, the configurator helps the internal order processing to ensure supply of the required products and components. It also allows older quotes to be picked up and updated to accommodate customers who have taken a long time to make the decision to buy the product. Sometimes the gap can be as long as a year during which the product designs or the component parts may have changed. With the intelligent configurator, the BoM can be updated easily and a new quote generated.

The overall impact of this is shorter and enhanced customer journeys – an objective that many digitalisation projects aim to achieve. In this case the time that it takes for the customer to interact with a technical sales consultant to specify their requirements is shortened. Additionally, the quality of product specification is improved because the right parts are ordered for the desired engine configuration. The automation reduces delays due to stock issues, for example the wrong parts being ordered, consequently avoiding delays in production and customer follow-up calls and support requirements. The improved speed of making a quote and having the specification done through to manufacturing the product has also given the company a competitive edge.

To summarise, the benefits include:

- shorter product configuration and quotation process;
- increased quality and accuracy of the BoM;
- shorter customer journeys from an initial interest in a product to a quote and then an order being placed;
- BoMs are linked up with product specification and engineering;
- improved internal order processing for parts and components and stock controls;
- easy to update older configurations to supply fresh quotes to clients;
- reduced time to train new technical sales consultants as the solution guides them through the options;
- increased availability of sales personnel.

Challenges

Initially, and unsurprisingly, the implementation team had some learning to do. This was more to do with the approach to knowledge transfer from experts to the solution than anything else. Engines are complex products and capturing information about parts and their dependencies from the expert engineers can be challenging.

The early approach saw product information captured at a detailed level before options at a higher level of decisions were clarified. This led to the solution diving into the details to produce the BoM quickly, which resulted in some errors as not all the constraints at higher levels or branches of the tree had been taken into account. Consequently, following a review, a more top-down approach was taken up to produce accurate BoMs. This was over 10 years ago and the solution has been operating reliably ever since.

Then there is the task of managing and maintaining the product information in the database as the company develops new products and responds to new regulatory and environmental requirements. This is an ongoing maintenance requirement rather than a challenge but it has to be factored in when building an intelligent configurator solution.

Under the hood of the solution

The CPQ solution uses symbolic AI to capture knowledge from experts to create constraints trees. The knowledge capture is done iteratively with the underlying technology using machine learning to induce a general decision tree that is then refined with further input from the expert. This includes capturing constraints and the consequences on the decisions resulting in a constraints tree that, combined with a database of product information, is used to guide the technical sales consultant through the process of engine configuration.

The sales consultants use the solution to configure the required features of the product in conversation with the client. As customers make their choices, the configuration is refined with advanced constraints inference from the trees ensuring that only valid features and attributes combinations are selectable. The BoM is produced at the end of the process.

The solution is based on Viabl.ai from XpertRule. The screenshot in Figure 8.1 shows a 'PC Product Configuration' knowledge base opened in the platform's knowledge base editor. The decision map shows the structure of the knowledge base for configuring the central processing unit (CPU) of the PC, while the editor pane (opened for the 'CPU' object) illustrates a truth table that shows all the possible decisions given the inputs, and an automatically induced decision tree generated from the table. This knowledge not only determines the CPU selection but also constrains the user at runtime from picking an invalid combination of values such as 'Cost'='High', 'Type'='Laptop', 'Usage'='Deep learning'. The runtime engine combines all these pieces of constraint knowledge to enforce the universal truth.

SUMMARY

Wärtsilä was an early adopter of AI for decision support. This case study has focused on its use of symbolic AI in sales optimisation in its marine and energy business. As a result the company has reduced lead times and can quickly generate quotes for complicated engines that are tailored to the customer's needs and preferences. This gives it a competitive edge as well as other benefits including better product configuration, improved internal ordering and stock control as well as smoother customer journeys.

Figure 8.1 An example of a decision map and the induced decision tree in a PC sale scenario

PART 3:
THE SHAPE OF THINGS TO COME – THE AUTONOMOUS ENTERPRISE

In Part 1 of the book I defined the concept of the autonomous enterprise, and gave an overview of the AI-powered technologies that are making it possible and the importance of the technologies' role in business innovation and efficiency. In Part 2, I provided a number of case studies to show examples of how AI can be applied in practice, be it in business or in healthcare, to provide both automation and augmentation as a decision-support tool. In Part 3, I focus on the concept of the autonomous enterprise, how we will get there, the enablers and what every organisation needs to consider and do as it journeys towards it.

9   THE AUTONOMOUS ENTERPRISE

In Part 1 of the book I described what AI is and how it can be used by enterprises for innovation and efficiency with use case examples provided throughout the early chapters. In Part 2 the case studies demonstrated the value that AI can generate for organisations in practice in real life. The applications were diverse and led to benefits that included more efficient processes, increased flexibility and capacity, augmented decision-making and improved outcomes. The case studies showed that organisations of all sizes can deploy AI and get benefits from it. They also highlighted that success comes with a mindset that is open and willing to try new ways of doing things, and textbook application of best practice in change management with a joined-up collaborative approach to introducing new technology, with pooling of knowledge and sharing resources.

In my view, all the emerging technologies, operational models, trends and the opportunities for innovation that I have covered in this book are combining to drive us towards the autonomous enterprise. In this chapter I delve into the concept of it, the journey towards it and how organisations can prepare for it.

THE START OF THE JOURNEY

Most organisations have already started their journeys to the autonomous enterprise by automating parts of their processes. In some industries companies are arguably further ahead than others, for example in the automotive industry where many processes have been extensively digitalised and robotised, particularly car manufacturing processes. Across industries, the trend is for more automation and one indicator is recent investments in technology. Figure 9.1 is from a study that I conducted in January 2021 at Emergence Partners (Burnett, 2021). As part of the study we interviewed senior decision-makers in 177 large enterprises in the US, UK, Germany, France and other major economies in Europe. We asked them what their technology investments had been in the previous 12 months. The chart in Figure 9.1 shows the top four investment priorities by industry. Importantly, it shows that automation was either the highest or joint highest priority for organisations in 7 out of 10 industries, with the automotive sector significantly ahead of others.

Automation changes how things are done in the enterprise. In fact, I would go further and say that it turns the traditional knowledge work inside out. Organisations need to prepare for this and adapt to ensure success. These are the subjects that I explore in the next few sections.

Figure 9.1 The top four enterprise technology investment priorities in 2020 by industry, based on interviews with decision-makers in 177 large organisations in Europe and the US

AUTONOMOUS ENTERPRISE DEFINITION

Before we delve deeper into the success factors for the autonomous enterprise, I would like to recap on the definition that I first provided in Chapter 1. The autonomous enterprise:

- Conducts its core daily business functions in a digital and automated manner with minimum human touchpoints, with AI embedded in many of its systems.

- Employs people but they will do fewer repetitive tasks such as checking and settling invoices, and more complex and strategic work, such as handling sensitive and complicated customer cases.

- Not only automates major operations but empowers staff to automate their own repetitive tasks as well. The autonomous enterprise provides IA and augmentation technologies to its staff to help them work more efficiently and productively. It also offers training and support to ensure that they can use those technologies effectively.

- Takes advantage of operational data to create digital twins – virtual models of some of its critical processes – to make sure that work flows through the organisation efficiently and that there are data available to support both automated and human decision-making.

- Not only analyses data to make better operational decisions, but to provide support for strategic decisions, and to manage the business and risks better and to innovate.

Examples of the transactional work that machines do within an autonomous enterprise include:

- data entry;
- checking huge numbers of documents for information;
- cross referencing and checking data for accuracy;
- answering simple and repetitive enquiries at any helpdesk or during customer interactions;
- capturing information, sourced both internally and externally, to analyse and create business intelligence reports;
- assessing cases to make decisions or to help humans make better decisions.

Examples of the higher value work that people do in an autonomous enterprise include:

- designing, implementing, overseeing and improving both automated and manual business processes;
- handling cases or enquiries that are too complex or sensitive for the AI to complete;
- planning and implementing routines for the AI to capture business intelligence from daily automated operations, and other sources of data both internal (e.g. widget sales data) and external (market trends);
- acting on the findings of analysis and reporting produced by AI to find opportunities for improving services, products and marketing and sales to increase revenue, some of this to support decision-making and problem solving in real time, for example if stocks are low in one location, finding surplus supplies elsewhere in the corporate network of warehouses thanks to analysis of stock data;
- accordingly, designing new products and services, planning business growth and geographic expansion and so on. These activities can be augmented with AI, for example 3D hand drawing visualisation tools for ideation and design concepts;
- managing the business and operations at team, division and corporate levels.

Examples of software tools that empower employees include:

- digital personal assistants that take dictation, arrange meetings and book conference rooms or calls on behalf of the worker;
- software that provides answers to their questions, for example based on team- or corporate-wide collaboration applications with shared insights and information;
- software that provides helpdesk and contact centre agents with:
  - best answers based on historical information – answers provided in the past to similar questions by their colleagues that have fully and satisfactorily answered customers' questions;
  - real-time and in context signposting to documents that show how similar requirements have been dealt with by the organisation before;

- analysis and reporting for decision support;
- automated work pattern insights and advice that can improve work–life balance for employees by optimising workloads and their fair distribution among team members, while increasing productivity;
- access to low- or no-code automation software to allow them to automate their repetitive tasks, provided together with training, hand-holding, governance and guiding frameworks.

Behind the definition that I have provided lies a whole series of good practices without which the autonomous enterprise would not be possible. I explore these later on in this chapter.

Another thing to note is that for new ventures it is easy to start out as an autonomous enterprise, with the latest automation technologies deployed from the beginning. Examples of this include Lemonade, the US-based insurance company that was set up from the start to run highly automated operations. It is not so easy to become an autonomous enterprise for established businesses with a mix of old and new systems.

It is not about ripping out old systems and replacing them with new ones in established organisations. For them there is a journey towards autonomy and that means incrementally automating suitable processes over a period of several years.

TURNING KNOWLEDGE PROCESSES INSIDE OUT

Knowledge work in organisations today is mostly conducted in a semi-automated fashion. There are software solutions such as ERP and line of business applications that bring a lot of business information together for knowledge workers to do their work. These include some automated information updates and calculations as well, and increasingly smarter help tools and best answers. In organisations, there are pools of people sitting in offices and using these solutions to do their jobs. The autonomous enterprise will change this model in that there will be pools of software on servers running in the cloud handling high-volume business transactions with people looking after them, guiding them or handling the exceptions that the machines cannot deal with. This is highlighted in Figure 9.2.

The change in the model of knowledge work will mean that enterprises will have to document not only processes but the expertise that they codify to create the automations. Maintaining the knowledge will be critical to allow processes to be conducted manually should a system failure happen, and to monitor the accuracy and efficiency of the codified operations. This is very important as with low-code development environments, experts can program their knowledge into software robots to create new automations and then move on to other jobs, leaving the organisation without the knowledge of how things are done except for the coding of the robot. Organisations will have to document their processes with full version control and life-cycle management to ensure that change can be managed along with the source code of their intelligent automations. Enterprises have to be able to roll back a version if a problem is encountered when it goes live.

Figure 9.2 Inside out knowledge work in the autonomous enterprise

Today's knowledge workers conduct business processes on their PCs using software on servers in the cloud.

Tomorrow's autonomous enterprise knowledge workers will supervise automation software robots and automated processes running on servers in the cloud and handle breakdowns and exceptions, as well as improve and update the automations.

Auditing and monitoring requirements will increase to ensure that processes are run correctly and that they comply with corporate policies and standards, and regulatory and ethical requirements, such as the EU's ethical guidelines for trustworthy AI (European Commission, 2019).

Training and knowledge transfer will have to be carefully managed for leavers and joiners and for succession planning and team career advancements. The managers of the future will mostly come from this pool of trained personnel and should gain good knowledge of how things are done as they come through the ranks.

Even some of these requirements can be automated, for example there are already technologies out there, such as process mining that I covered in Chapter 4, that capture process information and document it. Document management and software version and life-cycle control solutions have been around for decades.

The upshot of all of this is that we need to think about the transformation to autonomous enterprise and its impact on how we do things.

In the next sections I explore some of the characteristics of autonomous enterprises.

THE AUTONOMOUS ENTERPRISE MINDSET

While some organisations are very risk averse and avoid adopting new technologies, others embrace them. One example is Siemens GBS, which was the subject of the case study in Chapter 5. Although the case study was about its bionic agent, the company has been at the forefront of adopting advanced technology in many different ways, including the use of IA. Its leadership is happy to have new solutions trialled and with each one the organisation gains more skills and experiences.

The current wave of autonomous enterprises has emerged from this kind of mindset: organisations led by technology champions who are willing to try new ways of doing things. In this approach to adopting new technology, as in any others, it is important to manage the associated risks and capture the lessons learned to feed into future projects.

The autonomous enterprises that emerge from new ventures, those that bet big on intelligent technology from the start, will have the kind of mindset that will have moved well beyond concepts of recent decades such as digital- or automated-first. For them, automation is the norm.

While core business functions are automated as a strategic approach, the staff at all levels of the organisation are empowered to use technology to automate their own less interesting and transactional tasks. The organisation supports them by providing the technology, the training and the hand-holding that staff need to do this.

Starting with the end in mind

Adoption of AI should not be about having the latest new shiny thing but to achieve specific outcomes. In the Calderdale Council case study in Chapter 6 we saw clearly that the council started with the end in mind. The project was to improve customer services and to create capacity. Implementing VIRA, the IVA, was just one part of the bigger digitalisation project that saw an overhaul of the website and the introduction of smart forms. These work together well because they were all part of achieving a clear objective of increasing customer self-service with more digitalisation of services.

The joined-up, collaborative approach with pooling of resources

In the Calderdale Council case study we learnt of the organisation adopting AI as part of a bigger project, in which different ways of handling customer interactions were considered together in a joined-up approach. The same is true of the RBFT case study in Chapter 7. The deployment of the intelligent e-Stroke system was part of a bigger review of the complete stroke care pathway. The door-in-door-out model was not just improved by the introduction of the software but also the optimisation of some of the other steps in the pathway.

Joined-up working also involves collaboration with different teams, which can be inside or outside the organisation. In the Siemens GBS case study we learned that the organisation has a dedicated team that provides technology design and development services to its other departments. This helps it to keep skills in-house and develop new technology solutions as required. Another aspect of the development of the bionic agent was the organisation's desire to make it reusable. It designed the solution so that it could be repurposed and used for other requirements in the future. Accordingly, it captured and curated technology knowledge and know-how for reuse in the future.

The RBFT case study demonstrated how knowledge and CT scan data, shared among the TITAN network members, increased access to specialists and improved patient outcomes.

The theme of resource pooling was repeated in the Wärtsilä case study, with the company reducing its reliance on external consultancies by developing skills internally and creating a team that handles the development and maintenance of its intelligent CPQ solutions in-house.

Focus on phygital

The joined-up approach is particularly important when we look to joining up the digital and physical worlds. This is perhaps best illustrated with the example of car insurance. The easiest way to automate this is by providing quotes based on automated and intelligent risk assessments, and then accepting payments and processing the insurance policies online. In phygital the process can go further, for example if someone opts to have a car black box installed to get a reduced premium. While 90 per cent of the process of insuring the car could be automated, at some point there will need to be a handover to someone who is charged with sending the black box to the client and arranging for it be installed in their car. In a joined-up approach, the impact of automating the rest of the processes on the manual part would be assessed, risks such as black box supply and demand fluctuations taken into account and information about the state of risks shared with the intelligent solution that is involved in providing the quote. The system can then make decisions about the availability of the offer and inform the customer accordingly.

In contrast, in a disjointed approach, the customer would be offered cover at a discounted premium but the company might not be able to dispatch the black box for weeks due to supply issues, thus depriving itself of valuable driver data for insurance purposes.

Good data stewardship

Another aspect of joined-up work and essential for automation is good data management. Good practice is essential and with the help of intelligent technology, organisations can take analysis for decision support to new levels. In terms of good practice, we saw in the Calderdale case study in Chapter 6 that the council made extensive use of the data that it had from past chat conversations to train and enhance VIRA. It also gathered user feedback and captured operational data to monitor the performance of VIRA and to measure the quality of the customer experiences – it checked at what points customers dropped off, to get insights into what needed improving.

In the RBFT case study we saw another aspect of data stewardship and that was ensuring that the sharing of data with external partners was within data privacy requirements. The names of the patients were not visible in the shared scan images.

Good data stewardship is essential for AI and business automation. Today, organisations have data in hundreds of business systems on premises and on cloud. The data have to be maintained, their quality assured and updates propagated across systems to synchronise changes and ensure that operations run smoothly and that the organisation has a complete and accurate view of its key data, its golden records, such as customer and product data. Investment in data integration and quality assurance solutions is essential. These technologies are advancing fast and today it is possible to integrate swathes of business data to feed cognitive systems that can make automated predictions to advise decision-makers or make decisions automatically and execute processes accordingly. Some of the biggest companies, such as one of the largest consumer packaged goods (CPG) manufacturers in the world, are already using these types of systems.

Data-driven insights and innovation

The industry has been talking about analytics for decision support for decades. Machine learning is taking this capability to new levels, enabling more automated decision-making and process execution. Intelligent analytics enable budding autonomous enterprises to capture business critical data and apply analytics to get business and operational insights rapidly.

In Chapter 1, we learnt how Ocado, the UK online grocery store, conducts millions of demand and supply forecasts a day to ensure the freshness of its stock to minimise food waste. In its 2019 annual report (Ocado Group, 2019) it stated that it halved its food supply waste from 0.8 per cent to just 0.4 per cent of its sales. This is a double saving of costs and food waste.

In Chapter 3 we learnt how AI can help enterprises find the opportunity in a mass of data to improve something: one example is to use deep learning to run advanced analytics to gain insights on how your company is perceived by its customers. The analysis can provide insights over large populations or over long periods of time, to detect the likelihood of customers defecting to a competitor or defaulting on invoices. This would allow the organisation to make special offers to the clients or prepare to offer them a payment plan should it become necessary. Another opportunity is to analyse customer feedback on white goods and other products, either directly or by understanding the sentiment from comments posted on social media and to feed that information back to product engineering teams for enhancements.

Agility

Benjamin Franklin once said, 'In this world nothing can be said to be certain, except death and taxes.' I would add change to this list. Our world changes all the time, be it ecologically, environmentally, politically, socially or technologically. The latter faster than most of us can keep up with.

Change means that demand for products and services shift and alter. This changing pattern leads to some products and services having to be retired and new ones developed and brought to market. Businesses need agility to be able to move with the times and that ability is powered by data and information, for example where the issues and bottlenecks are in their organisations or what to change in response to new requirements. Data captured from automated operations can provide these insights. We saw a great example of this in the Calderdale Council case study where the contact centre staff were trained to add new vocabulary to VIRA and teach it to deal with conversations in new contexts so that the council could answer additional customer questions. Over the COVID-19 pandemic this capability has helped the organisation to deal with changes that the UK Government mandates, often at short notice, many relating to new rules for lockdowns, self-testing and isolation, in schools, in social care and more. This is agility in practice, an important facet of the autonomous enterprise.

It is also important to keep an eye on emerging technology and global trends to prepare for the longer term. It helps to always keep aspirations going and visualising the shape of things to come; how emerging technological developments might impact the organisation, and what it would need to do to be ready for that future.

THE ONGOING AUTONOMOUS ENTERPRISE JOURNEY

While many organisations have already automated some of their business processes and operations, new developments will bring fresh opportunities for innovation. Take the automotive industry – car manufacturing processes have been highly automated with robots assembling car parts to create specific models and customised version of cars to order. The robots receive their instructions from microchips that have been preloaded with the build data or they get the information downloaded to them.

Customers can choose the car configuration that they want when they order the car and these days most of the configuration work is done on a self-service basis with intelligent CPQ solutions taking the customers through an array of options such as engine type, wheels, interior materials and trims, information and entertainment systems and so on. The choices are captured and used to create the product specification that is sent to manufacturing – loaded onto a chip for a largely automated manufacturing process to get started.

But what if it became possible to take the automation further, for example allowing the finished car to be automatically loaded onto a truck for delivery to the customer? What if the lorry could be replaced by an autonomous one to drive and deliver the car to the customer at home? What if the car itself was autonomous and could actually drive itself to the customer's house? This would bring benefits to the manufacturer, the customer and the environment. It would mean:

- The customer doesn't have to make a journey to the showroom to pick up the car, cutting out associated energy consumption and power generation fumes for travelling there.

- The need for buying a forklift or a robot for loading the car onto a lorry would not be necessary, reducing investment requirements in machinery, cutting demand and reducing their manufacture and associated industrial waste.

- A lorry, be it manual or autonomous, would not be required to deliver the car to the customer, consequently reducing demand for lorries and the industrial waste that their manufacturing produces.

Figure 9.3 provides an overview of car buying scenarios today and in future.

These kinds of scenarios are closer to becoming reality than we think; firstly, there is RAY the robot at Dusseldorf Airport that parks cars with great accuracy. It loads them onto a car-sized platform on wheels using a forklift truck mechanism and deposits them in parking bays (Shadbolt, 2015). There are also trials of autonomous vehicles going on in many cities around the world: Oxford (Browne, 2020) and Birmingham (Stone, 2021) in the UK, for instance.

Figure 9.3 Car buying processes today and possibilities for automation in future

Scenario 1: The customer orders a car. The car is manufactured and taken to a show room where the customer picks it up and drives it away.

Scenario 2: The customer orders a car. The car is manufactured and is manually loaded to a lorry, driven by a driver who delivers the car to the customer's home.

Scenario 3: The customer orders a car. The car is manufactured and loaded by a robot to an autonomous lorry that delivers the car to the customer's home.

Scenario 4: The customer orders a car. The car is manufactured and autonomously drives itself to the customer's home. This scenario optimises the car delivery model by reducing journeys and cutting out the need to invest in forklifts and lorries.

The point that I am making here is that, no matter in what industry you operate, even in the highly automated automotive industry, there will be other opportunities for automation that will become possible. This is about thinking of possibilities and innovating, with the people in the organisation continuously monitoring emerging technology trends to provide the ideas, the planning and the development of the next leading-edge capability.

HOW THINGS CAN GO WRONG

There are many organisations that have introduced automation in parts of their operations but in a disjointed way that can create problems for both the company and its customers. For example, can you imagine the hurt that a customer would feel if tickets to a much anticipated gig by a favourite band that they had booked as part of a phygital marketing offer never materialised? It would take an awful lot of time and grovelling to the customer by the company to make up for that kind of let-down.

There is much more that can go wrong, from simply badly designed online user interfaces to inadequate integration between systems that prevent employees doing their jobs well. I examine some of these factors in this section. These are well-known issues by veterans of the IT industry because they cause problems for organisations all the time today. They would do so for autonomous enterprises of the future as well if not addressed.

Old and disjointed systems

One of the biggest problems in enterprises stem from their lack of investment in technology modernisation. Systems need to be kept up to date and their lifetimes managed so that over time they can be replaced with new ones with better features and connections to other systems. The lack of investment results in organisations relying on old and bloated systems – full of out-of-date data – that make it hard for employees to do their work. Problems faced by staff include not being able to find the correct customer record due to duplicated records, or incomplete product information that is out of synch with the latest models and offerings, as well as outdated information about the customer and their purchase history. These types of problems lead to a lack of job satisfaction among staff and increased attrition rates.

Outdated software systems that are no longer supported by their manufacturers can be cybersecurity hazards because vendors typically enhance their software security in the updates that they release. Older systems leave known vulnerabilities open to use by hackers.

Poor data integration

Older systems are difficult to integrate with other systems and that means that data cannot easily be maintained and synchronised between them. This results in problems such as out-of-date customer and product information, making it hard for the company to deliver its services and deal with customer enquiries smoothly. Not looking after data leads to more problems, such as mistakes when undertaking business processes. If you automate a process with poor data then, as the speed of processing increases, the data problem gets propagated through more transactions and to more systems, with chaos ensuing.

Poor customer experience

We have all experienced poorly designed websites and apps – those that leave us going round and round on websites but never finding the information that we are looking for. The same thing can happen with chatbots or IVAs that are poorly trained with limited understanding of the subject matter that they are supposed to be able to handle. Similarly, phone switchboard options can take you through many topics except the one that you are looking for, and then a recorded voice may well advise you to visit the website and hang up on you. These are badly designed customer journeys. They have been created without the customer perspective – not seeing the journey through the eyes of the customer – leading to unnecessary contact by phone and other channels. These types of issues lead to a lot of customer dissatisfaction.

Inadequate staff training

Another problem is implementing highly advanced systems but failing to adequately train staff to use them. This means that some staff will find it difficult to do their work and some will even try to bypass the system. There are examples of this where, instead of putting information into the provided system, members of a team have used spreadsheets for their personal use. The spreadsheets are not shared and leave other staff in the team in the dark about the cases that their colleagues have been working on. This means that they cannot answer any questions about the case work and are not able to address any issues that might arise when those colleagues are not in the office.

This kind of practice leads to a growing problem of 'shadow IT', which is when employees use software applications outside recommended practices and IT policies, including accessing unapproved apps remotely on cloud. As well as limiting collaboration, the reduced levels of visibility and auditability of process steps and decisions can lead to risks such as failure to comply with regulatory requirements and information quality and security issues.

In a contact centre, this type of scenario would mean that staff are not able to use the systems that are there to provide the information that they need to answer customers' questions. Imagine being on the phone to an unhappy client and not being able to use the system that would allow you to help them. As the agent, you would get more and more flustered and to keep the customer happy, you might make them a special offer that you cannot provide, leading to further customer dissatisfaction.

My personal experience of how things can go wrong

Without a joined-up approach, and use of automation in this data-heavy phygital world, things can go very wrong. An example of a scenario to be avoided is the terrible experience that I had a couple of years ago when I contacted my mobile phone operator to upgrade my plan.

I had three existing devices supplied to me by the company, only one of which was a phone with a number that I was well familiar with. Unbeknown to me, the company allocated phone numbers to the other two devices as well, even though they were not mobile phones. With similar pricing and usage patterns, it was not possible for me to identify which was which on my phone bills either. When I phoned to discuss upgrade options with the phone operator, I found that the contact centre agent could not tell me which phone number was allocated to which device either. There was no information on her system that linked the phone number to the device type – phone, dongle, tablet and so on. That made the upgrade discussion difficult because she expected me to give her information that the company had not supplied me.

She did not have easy access to the latest product stock information either and took several minutes to check the relevant databases. Having finally checked the product portfolio and stock databases, she told me that the model of the phone that I wanted was not available but she would send me the next model up on a complimentary basis. She also said that she would send me two new SIM cards, one for my phone and one for one of the other devices that I was also upgrading. The instruction that I got was that once I received the SIM cards I should go on the website and activate each SIM. When I asked her how to do this she told me that I had to put the phone number for each device in the activation field of the SIM web page. I explained to her that the second device was not a phone and I did not know its phone number but she could not help me with that.

Needless to say that a painful sequence of activating SIMs by trial and error followed that went on for several days, leading to a number of replacement SIM cards having to be dispatched to me, my third device getting disconnected unnecessarily and having to be reconnected with a new SIM card. It was a long and painful customer journey for me, having to make many calls to the phone company, put up with their long waiting times and listen to the painful music that they played while I waited on the phone. Each call was picked up by a different agent who had similar issues:

- They had poor data:
  - The information that I had been given by the operator about the products that I had was incomplete.
  - The way that the data had been stored was inadequate, that is, the phone numbers that were stored in my records did not show the types of devices that I had.
  - The product catalogue was out of date – at first, it showed that the model that I wanted was out of stock, but later someone in the organisation managed to find one and send it to me.
- Poor system performance:
  - Either their databases were slow to respond, leaving agents and customer waiting for minutes on live calls
  - or they had not provided sufficient training to their staff to enable them to use the systems to get the information that they needed to answer their customers' questions.

119

- Disjointed automation:
  - While some aspects of the service were partially automated, for example SIM activation, the rest of the processes were manual and disjointed. Clearly there were no links between customer information, product catalogues, stocks and the information needed for SIM activation.
- The operations led to staff dissatisfaction:
  - This disjointed set of phone, online and manual steps made the service wholly inadequate, leading not just to customer dissatisfaction but to feelings of anxiety and frustration by staff.
  - Even their customer complaint team could not raise much enthusiasm to deal with the complaint that I made following my horrible experience – clearly I was one of many dissatisfied customers they had had that day – there were no follow-ups.

When my new phone arrived, I discovered that it was the model that I had asked for originally and not the complementary upgrade to the next best product that I had been promised. I had received no communication about this and felt seriously let down by the company.

They failed to notify me of the change in the model that they supplied me – basically the special offer that the contact centre agent had made me could not be fulfilled and no explanation was offered as to why.

This completely negated the goodwill that they had shown when the agent made me the offer of a better model.

This company had significant information problems, but many of these could have been resolved by automation:

- product catalogue and stock levels updated automatically in real time, and the information uploaded to a system that the contact centre agents had access to and that worked fast in real time;
- product types added as a field to the database of phone numbers that were used for device identification;
- notifications of changes to orders sent automatically.

There is really no excuse for this kind of poor service, even if an organisation is full of legacy systems that are difficult to upgrade and integrate. Leading companies have shown that the use of IA technologies such as RPA with IDP can fill the integration gap between systems, help with process automation and ensure data accuracy and quality.

In the case of my mobile phone operator, an apology for poor service should have been sent automatically as well but there were no apologies and no follow-ups.

SUMMARY

In this chapter I covered the autonomous enterprise in detail and described the factors that help organisations with their journeys to becoming one. I highlighted the need for joined-up and well thought out automation that provides good experiences for both customers and staff. The journey will be never-ending as new technologies emerge and enable us to do more. I highlighted this in the car manufacturing scenario to show how even an advanced industry in terms of enterprise autonomy cannot stand still.

Finally, I looked at how things can go wrong and the factors that contribute to them, including legacy systems, poor system integration, out-of-date information and inadequate training of staff. I shared my first-hand experience of poor service by a mobile phone operator that I believe was caused by all of these factors.

In the next chapter I discuss the future of jobs and the ethics of technology.

10 AUTOMATION AND SOCIETY

In this chapter I look at the impact of automation on employment in the past and extrapolate to suggest the likely impact in the future. This discussion about jobs leads to a more general discussion about ethics and the way that AI can be applied for the good of society.

JOBS FOR HUMANS

The elephant in the room is the question of jobs for humans. What is going to be the impact of automation of work on the jobs landscape and society as a whole? These are complex questions that cannot be answered easily, given that in the jobs market there are other factors at work.

While the jobs market varies by country, we can gain some insights by looking at the statistics in the UK. Firstly, nearly a quarter of the population is over 60 according to the Office for National Statistics (ONS) (ONS, 2021a). The effect of the aging population is showing in rising vacancies for jobs such as lorry drivers. There are not enough young people coming through to take up the vacancies as those approaching retirement in the existing workforce leave the sector. This is leading to a serious shortage of drivers that is affecting the supply chain in the country. This pattern is likely to be repeated in other industries as well.

Macro factors also impact the market. For example, job vacancies in the UK dropped and unemployment went up in 2020, early in the pandemic, but because of Brexit and COVID-19, many EU workers left the country. This means that at the time of writing, there is a gaping hole in skills in some sectors in the UK including, but not limited to, healthcare and veterinary medicine, agriculture, hospitality and tourism, construction and transport.

Another finding from a study by the UK Government, called 'Guidance – Trend Deck 2021: Skills' (UK Government, 2020) published in June 2021, shown in Figure 10.1, indicates that vacancies are becoming more and more difficult to fill due to lack of qualifications, relevant skills or experience. Skill-shortage vacancies comprised nearly a quarter of all vacancies in 2019 (24 per cent, up from 22 per cent in the 2013–17 period). The skill-shortage density is highest in construction (36 per cent, the same as 2017) and manufacturing (36 per cent, up from 29 per cent in 2017).

Figure 10.1 Number and density of skill-shortage vacancies (SSVs), by sector

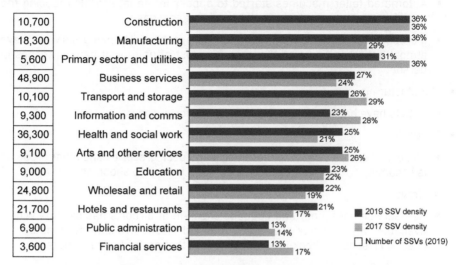

Base: All establishment vacancies (range: public admin. and retail 3,584)

At the same time, in 2019, the ONS in the UK conducted a study, 'Which occupations are at highest risk of being automated?' (ONS, 2019), that estimated that 7.4 per cent of jobs were at high risk of being lost due to automation. The estimate had dropped from 8.1 per cent to 7.4 per cent between 2011 and 2017. The agency surmised that the need for skills for more complex jobs had increased over this period and these were jobs that were more difficult to automate.

The implication of these studies is unsurprising; skills are very much in demand and skilled jobs have a low likelihood of getting automated. They are very likely to continue to provide opportunities for work. Clearly measures are needed by governments and industries to help people get the skills that are in demand, not only to fill current vacancies but to help maintain employment against the backdrop of increasing automation. The more opportunities we create for people to develop skills, the better we mitigate risks of increasing unemployment because of automation.

It is not all about existing jobs though, because throughout history we have seen new jobs being created while others have disappeared. I cover this in more detail next.

CREATION OF NEW ROLES

In addition to the current skills shortage, another factor to consider is the creation of new jobs. If you look back at history, many different kinds of jobs emerged and then disappeared due to automation or changes in lifestyles. White goods, for example, have automated our home chores to a degree, reducing the need for domestic staff. Farming has been mechanised and automated to a large degree, reducing the need for hundreds of farm workers. We can see the trend for mechanisation and digitalisation of work continuing in many different industries, such as:

- Banking:
  - Automated teller machines started to appear in the late 1970s reducing the need for people to go inside bank branches to get cash.
  - Increased levels of self-service such as app-based banking services have almost entirely eliminated the need for most of us to visit bank branches in person.
- Manufacturing:
  - Robots have been building cars in factories for decades.
- Retail:
  - The use of robots in warehouses to pick and pack groceries and other products is becoming widespread, fuelled by demand for online shopping.
- Air travel:
  - Self-service passenger and baggage check-in at airports has become widely available with typically only a few manned kiosks available to handle self-check-in issues or check-in any passengers that prefer to do it in person.

These automations that have developed in the past 50 years are only examples of the bigger picture of increased uses of computers and digitalisation of business processes and self-service using online channels. The increasing levels of computerisation and automation of work have not led to mass unemployment for humans to date. This is indicated by data from the ONS (ONS, 2021b) that show employment rates in the UK today are at similar levels to 50 years ago in the 1970s, having gone through waves of change in between due to economic recessions. This is highlighted in Figure 10.2.

Figure 10.2 UK unemployment rate (aged 16 and over, seasonally adjusted) (Source: ONS, 2021b)

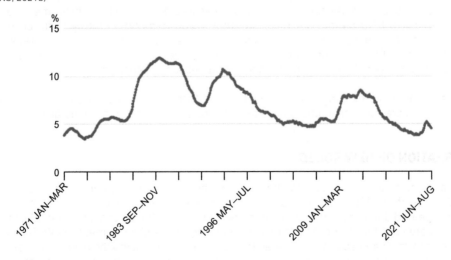

The US unemployment figures compiled by the US Bureau of Labor Statistics (2021) tell a similar story. They show the impact of the pandemic but that the rate is returning to a pre-pandemic level and to a similar rate to 20 years ago in 2001, as shown in Figure 10.3.

Figure 10.3 US civilian unemployment rate (the shaded area represents recession, as determined by the US National Bureau of Economic Research)

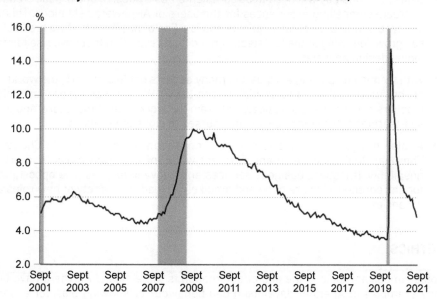

I believe one reason for today's low unemployment rate, despite existing levels of computerisation and automation of office work, is that new jobs have been created – and it is likely that they will continue to be created as seen over past centuries. New jobs in recent times have included social media marketing roles, industry research and analysis, drone pilots and building energy assessors and certifiers. At the same time, because of our changing lifestyles and work models, be it due to the pandemic, increased availability of technology or political developments such as Brexit, vacancies in some sectors have rocketed, for example delivery drivers and warehouse workers. Accordingly, we are likely to see new jobs and growing employment in some sectors offset job losses due to AI-enabled automation of knowledge work. Examples of where new roles are likely to be created include: the environment sector where demand for skills is likely to go up as we search for new solutions and services to help mitigate risks and the impact of global warming; the space race, which is hotting up with demand for skills to take the human race to other planets for research as well as for future commerce and tourism. This is likely to lead to more skilled work opportunities albeit in small numbers, but it is an indication of how new jobs will be created with advances in science and technology

AI will augment many of the jobs mentioned above and help by boosting analysis of data and identification of potential solutions.

It is important to note that because AI leads to more changes in our work and lifestyles and creates new models for business, it is likely to create new jobs itself (and in fact it has been doing so with roles such as AI supervisors and data scientists):

- In the technology sector, we will need more skills to build all the technology, machines and robots that we are likely to need, to maintain them and manage their life cycles.

- Skills in technology will need to be complemented by design and artistic creativity to create compelling experiences for the users of AI-powered solutions. This will increase demand for creative people and is a line of business that we are likely to see grow, following in the footsteps of the digital revolution that gave rise to many digital design agencies.

- With technology playing a big part in many aspects of life and work, the workforce of the future will need to be highly tech-savvy. We will need more technology teachers and lecturers to educate and train the workforce of the future, and to aid self-learning by creating new online courses to close the skills gap.

- AI also brings great opportunities for innovation, as mentioned in Chapter 3. The opportunities cover many different walks of life, from music and arts to hospitality, transport, business services and heavy industries. The opportunities for entrepreneurship are huge and are likely to lead to a variety of new roles and vacancies.

AI ETHICS

Another important topic in the age of automation is the ethics of AI. There have been many examples of AI either developing bad behaviour or showing bias, for example Microsoft's Tay (Griffin, 2016) that learnt bad behaviour from Twitter conversations and had to be shut down after it made offensive tweets. As another example, some facial recognition software was found to be poor at correctly recognising women and people of colour, and some algorithms led to biased decisions being made against people of colour or people from underprivileged backgrounds in different settings, such as assessment for parole in the US and student assessments in the UK.

Problems with AI can happen in many different ways, including:

- Poor design and enhancement decisions – this could lead to substandard interfaces that can deprive some users from being able to use the product, or build exclusion or prejudicial bias into the software.

- Inadequate training data that are not representative of the population that it is targeting, for example not enough samples of women's faces to train AI for facial recognition. This can lead to errors or biased decisions automatically made by AI when it goes live.

- Inadequate testing against a wide variety of use cases and user scenarios, consequently not effectively mitigating risks.

- Opaque decision-making by AI that cannot be explained – this is leading to demand for explainable AI that is necessary to show fairness and also compliance with regulatory requirements, for example in healthcare and financial services. Vendors are working on addressing this type of issue, for example I know one NLP vendor that allows the user to trace decisions made by the software to the training that the AI received so that issues can become visible and be addressed.

In the wrong hands AI can be used maliciously for many purposes, from cybercrime to controlling human lives.

A report titled 'The malicious use of artificial intelligence: Forecasting, prevention, and mitigation' (Brundage et al., 2018), written by a group of experts from different academic and research institutes including the universities of Oxford and Cambridge and the Open AI foundation, explores the potential risks of malicious AI in great detail and calls for prevention and risk mitigation.

The report identifies risks such as AI making it easier for bad actors to undertake more automated and highly targeted cybercrime, or create new types of attacks that explore the vulnerabilities of AI systems, for example where they rely on human speech synthesis and the risks of impersonation. Other risks include AI used for autonomous weapons and political surveillance. The report challenges policymakers to collaborate with the technology industry to mitigate risks. It calls for researchers and developers to consider the dual nature of their work and the risks that it might lead to, seriously. It highlights the need for best practice and involvement of a range of stakeholders and domain experts in the discussion.

The good news is that we can develop good AI to fight the bad. For example, AI is already being used to provide predictive and preventative cyber protection for enterprise systems. However, we cannot ignore the threat of malicious AI and must act to prevent it effectively. Governments are starting to act, for example the EU has already outlined a series of guiding principles for ethical AI (Madiega, 2019) and it is set to follow with more action.

The industry is starting to act too. For example, guidance is emerging from institutions such as the Institute of Electrical and Electronics Engineers (IEEE) in the US, which has recently published guidance in a paper titled 'A call to action for businesses using AI' (IEEE, 2020) that includes an AI ethics readiness framework. The Future of Life Institute has published the 'Asilomar AI principles' (The Future of Life Institute, 2017). These are 23 guiding principles for AI development and application.

Software tools and methodologies to help remove bias from algorithms are also emerging. These address aspects such as bias in data and personal data privacy. There are tools that check and certify AI software for cybersecurity resilience and protection against tampering and hacking.

This is an emerging field and much still needs to be done to educate the industry's workforce and to raise awareness about poor software development practices that can lead to problems in the finished product.

ETHICAL TECHNOLOGY

While much attention is focused on AI, very little has been said about the ethics in technology as a whole. I believe strongly that we should take into account technology as a whole and not just AI. For example, the majority of mobile phone users did not or still do not know about tracking and information sharing by apps. When Apple introduced its App Tracking Transparency to let users know, 85 per cent said no to tracking (Appleyard, 2021). This kind of tracking is not an AI problem but a bigger technology issue. Tracking of user activity is just one of the problems with seemingly harmless apps that billions of us have downloaded on our phones. Location tracking is particularly bad and has already started to eat into people's privacy in harmful ways. There is the case of the priest, a top US Catholic Church official, who was outed by the Catholic press that learnt from location tracking apps on his phone that he was visiting gay bars. According to *The Washington Post* he has had to resign (Boorstein, Iati and Shin, 2021). The consequences of such a capability enabled by a seemingly harmless app on a phone are huge. It is not just the loss of privacy but increased physical risks for people, for women with abusive partners for example.

This example illustrates one of the many reasons why we should work towards ethical technology and not just AI. This is why in 2020, at Emergence Partners, I created the Ethics in Technology Assessment (ETA) framework (Burnett, 2020) to help technology vendors assess the state of ethics in their organisations to identify any gaps and risks, and plan remedial action.

AI FOR GOOD

The potential of AI for good should not be overshadowed by the possibility of its malicious use. I highlighted the use of AI to reduce energy consumption in industrial plants in Chapter 1. Another example in Chapter 4 was how AI is starting to help the elderly in their homes. AI to improve patient outcomes in stroke care was the subject of the RBFT case study in Chapter 7. These and more examples are highlighted in Figure 10.4.

The examples that I have provided in Figure 10.4 help with the United Nations' 17 sustainable development goals (United Nations, n.d.). These include:

- zero hunger;
- good health and well-being;
- reduced inequalities;
- climate action;
- life on land;
- peace, justice and strong institutions.

We can accelerate the achievement of the goals with AI but must actively follow good risk mitigation strategies that include well considered development using best practice

Figure 10.4 Examples of AI for good

AI is emerging as an intelligent and dynamic survey tool that can help with mediation to get consensus and bring divided communities together in conflict zones.

AI for weed control in farming, helps to reduce the use of chemicals and costs.

AI helps with treatment of stroke patients by providing CT scan image analysis and decision support to physicians. It is being used in this way in many countries including the UK and Germany.

AI can reduce the carbon footprint of heavy industries with plant-wide monitoring and intelligent controls leading to optimisation of energy consumption.

Trials of AI to help the elderly and the vulnerable with voice commands and physical robots are showing good progress.

Autonomous vehicles will help transport people who are not physically able to drive and particularly those living in remote locations.

and continuous monitoring and assessing of intelligent systems and the outcomes that they deliver. In this way we can ensure that the development of AI is sustainable as well.

Another point is that it is through advances in AI for cybersecurity that we can fight its malicious use in cyber and political spheres. AI to find and highlight misinformation spread via social media is already being trialled and more developments are sure to follow.

SUMMARY

The future of jobs is a very important issue that we need to address as enterprises become increasingly more autonomous. While automation will reduce the number of jobs in some organisations, other forces are at work that will continue to fuel the jobs market. Firstly, the aging population indicates that vacancies will continue to increase in some industries. Secondly, insights from the UK ONS and the Government indicate the rising importance of skills, with many skilled vacancies proving hard to fill. Thirdly, another study by the ONS indicates that some low-skilled jobs are more likely to get automated than others. These findings point to the importance of helping people to gain the skills that are in demand to mitigate risks of unemployment.

History has shown us how as some jobs disappeared over the centuries, new ones came about. That pattern is likely to continue in the future with demand for AI solutions creating new roles in its own right. Both growing and burgeoning industries such as technology, space exploration and tourism are also set to create more demand for human workers.

Government and industry players are starting to address the issue of AI ethics. This is needed to ensure fair outcomes from AI. The risk from malicious uses of AI cannot be ignored. While good AI applications are being developed to counter some of the threats, action is needed by governments and the industry to mitigate them.

I believe that the focus on ethics of AI alone is insufficient to address the bigger problem of ethics of technology as a whole, such as abuse of mobile phone data. The whole field needs to come under scrutiny and good practice guidance provided and embedded across the industry.

These are exciting times for AI in the world. We need to learn from our past mistakes, such as allowing unethical sharing and use of people's personal data by mobile apps, to guide AI development along an ethical path.

AFTERWORD

To date, the concept of the autonomous enterprise has not been talked about much by the technology industry. This is because we are still in the early stages of automating knowledge work and some of the enabling technologies are very new. However, I believe that my concept of the autonomous enterprise very much describes the shape of things to come.

As AI technology advances and levels of automation of office work increase, and the shift of focus from digital to phygital goes on, we will see more and more autonomous enterprises emerging in the world, with work, real life and virtual experiences getting transformed over time.

We are already at the beginning of this journey and it is important that we learn how best to make the trip, so we do not repeat the mistakes of the past, such as the personal data abuse fiascos that have happened all too often, and the inadvertent creation of new dangers and threats. If we do this well, we might be able to hand the Earth to future generations in a better state.

The way that we work will change and that needs to be managed to ensure resilient enterprises. Organisations will need to prepare for the change and be willing to adopt new operating models that are likely to emerge with increasing enterprise autonomy. Furthermore, the ethics of AI need to be managed and there is no time like the present for governments, the technology industry and users of technology to act to ensure that AI is developed and applied ethically and fairly. It is also important to develop good AI to mitigate the risks of the malicious use.

AI gives us great potential to innovate. In my mind, this is one of the most important aspects of it. Accordingly, my final recommendation to you is to go forth and innovate with AI.

I hope I have inspired you to examine the opportunities that are out there for your organisation and along the path to enterprise autonomy. I wish you all the best with your journey.

REFERENCES

Amazon (n.d.) Amazon SageMaker. Available from https://aws.amazon.com/sagemaker/

Apple (n.d. (a)) Apple Neural Engine wiki. Available from https://apple.fandom.com/wiki/Neural_Engine

Apple (n.d. (b)) CoreML. Available from https://developer.apple.com/machine-learning/core-ml/

Appleyard, B. (2021) Apple vs Facebook – Silicon Valley's new cold war. *New Statesman.* 16 July. p. 22.

Arnold, Z., Rahkovsky, I. and Huang, T. (2020) *Tracking AI Investment.* Washington DC: Center for Security and Emerging Technology.

Blake, D. S. (2021) Ocado Group blog. *Ocado Group.* 27 July. Available from https://www.ocadogroup.com/technology/blog/how-we-improve-forecasting-and-availability-neural-networks-and-deep-learning

Boorstein, M. Iati, M. and Shin, A. (2021) Top U.S. Catholic Church official resigns after cellphone data used to track him on Grindr and to gay bars. *The Washington Post.* 21 July. Available from https://www.washingtonpost.com/religion/2021/07/20/bishop-misconduct-resign-burrill/

Bornet, P., Barkin, I. and Wirtz, J. (2020) *Intelligent Automation – Welcome to the World of HYPERAUTOMATION.* Published by the authors. Great Britain: Amazon.

Browne, D. (2020) Oxford to begin live trials of autonomous vehicles. *Transport Network.* 22 October. Available from www.transport-network.co.uk/Oxford-to-begin-live-trials-of-autonomous-vehicles/16916

Brundage, M. et al. (2018) The malicious use of artificial intelligence: Forecasting, prevention, and mitigation. Future of Humanity Institute, University of Oxford, Centre for the Study of Existential Risk, University of Cambridge, Center for a New American Security, Electronic Frontier Foundation, Open AI. Available from https://arxiv.org/pdf/1802.07228.pdf

Burnett, S. (2019) Five AI advancements that are making intelligent automation more intelligent. *Information Age.* 11 July. Available from www.information-age.com: https://www.information-age.com/intelligent-automation-sarah-burnett-123483950/

Burnett, S. (2020) Ethics in Technology Assessment (ETA). *Emergence.* Available from https://emergencehq.com/ethics-in-technology-assessment/

Burnett, S. (2021) Technology impact pulse survey report Q1 2021. London: Emergence Partners.

Care at Home using Intelligent Robotic Omni-function Nodes (CHIRON) (n.d.) Available from https://chiron.org.uk/

Cockburn, I. M., Henderson, R. and Stern, S. (2018) The impact of artificial intelligence on innovation. *National Bureau of Economic Research*. Available from https://www.nber.org/papers/w24449

Dahlquist, E. (2020) Plant-wide monitoring and control of data-intensive processes with AI functions. *Open Access Government*. 2 October. Available from https://www.openaccessgovernment.org/plant-wide-monitoring-and-control-of-data-intensive-processes-with-ai-functions/95449/

Deep AI (n.d.) ReLu. Available from https://deepai.org/machine-learning-glossary-and-terms/relu

DeepMind (2020) Using Unity to help solve intelligence. London: DeepMind. Available from https://arxiv.org/pdf/2011.09294.pdf

European Commission (2019) Ethics guidelines for trustworthy AI. 8 April. Available from https://digital-strategy.ec.europa.eu/en/library/ethics-guidelines-trustworthy-ai

European Union (2020) White paper on artificial intelligence – A European approach to excellence and trust. Brussels: European Union. Available from https://ec.europa.eu/info/sites/default/files/commission-white-paper-artificial-intelligence-feb2020_en.pdf

Eurostat (2021) Recent job starters by economic activity in the EU, Q2 2021. 22 October. Available from https://ec.europa.eu/eurostat/en/web/products-eurostat-news/-/ddn-20211022-1

Everest Group (2020) *Enterprise Intelligent Automation Adoption Maturity | Pinnacle Model Analysis.* Dallas: Everest Group.

Facebook Prophet (n.d.) Prophet. Available from https://facebook.github.io/prophet/

Feng, J. and Shengnan, L. (2019). Performance analysis of various activation functions in neural networks. *IOP Conference Series: Journal of Physics*. 1237 022030. Available from https://iopscience.iop.org/article/10.1088/1742-6596/1237/2/022030

FUDIPO (2016) Available from https://fudipo.eu: https://fudipo.eu/whats-fudipo/

Griffin, A. (2016) Tay tweets: Microsoft apologises for robot's racist and genocidal tweets. *The Independent*. 27 March. Available from https://www.independent.co.uk/life-style/gadgets-and-tech/news/tay-tweets-microsoft-apologises-for-robot-s-racist-and-genocidal-tweets-a6955056.html

HM Revenue and Customs (2020) *Personal Tax Credits Statistics: Child and Working Tax Credits Error and Fraud Statistics 2018–19, first release.* Liverpool: HM Revenue and Customs.

IDC (2020a) *Market Perspective Toward the AI-Powered Contact Center.* Needham: International Data Corporation (IDC).

IDC (2020b) *IDC FutureScape: Worldwide Artificial Intelligence 2021 Predictions.* Needham: International Data Corporation (IDC).

IEEE (2020) *A Call to Action for Businesses Using AI.* Piscataway, NJ: IEEE.

Image-net.org (2014) Imagenet Large Scale Visual Recognition Challenge 2014 (ILSVRC2014). Available from image-net.org: http://image-net.org/challenges/LSVRC/2014/

Keras (n.d.) Getting started. Available from https://keras.io/

Lee, C.-S. (2001) An analytical framework for evaluating e-commerce business models and strategies. Bradford: MCB University Press.

Lillicrap, D. G. (2018) Measuring abstract reasoning in neural networks. Stockholm: DeepMind.

Lowe, A. and Lawless, S. (2020) *Artificial Intelligence Foundations – Learning from Experience.* Swindon: BCS.

Madiega, T. (2019) *EU Guidelines on Ethics.* Strasbourg: European Union.

Markoff, J. (2014) Computer eyesight gets a lot more accurate. *The New York Times.* 18 August. Available from https://bits.blogs.nytimes.com/2014/08/18/computer-eyesight-gets-a-lot-more-accurate/

Microsoft Azure (n.d.) Azure Cognitive Services. Available from https://azure.microsoft.com/en-gb/services/cognitive-services/

Mukerji, P. (2019) *The Impact of Algorithmic Trading in a Simulated Asset Market.* Basel: MDPI.

Nagaratnam, D. K. (2020) *Implementing AI in Stroke Pathway: Local and Regional Experience.* Presentation deck by Dr Kiruba Nagaratnam, Clinical Lead for Stroke Medicine, Royal Berkshire NHS FT, Clinical Lead (Acute), BOB ISDN, Reading.

National Audit Office (2019) Submission to the UK 2019 local government finance and 2019 spending review. London: UK Parliament. Available from https://publications.parliament.uk/pa/cm201719/cmselect/cmcomloc/2036/203605.htm

Natural Language Toolkit (n.d.) Natural Language Toolkit. Available from NLTK 3.5 documentation at https://www.nltk.org/

Ocado Group (2019) Changing the way the world shops, Ocado Group Plc annual report and accounts. For the 52 weeks ended 1 December 2019. Hatfield: Ocado Group.

Ocado Group (2020) Ocado Group plc annual report. Hatfield: Ocado Group.

Office for National Statistics (ONS) (2019) Which occupations are at highest risk of being automated? 25 March. Available from https://www.ons.gov.uk/employmentandlabourmarket/peopleinwork/employmentandemployeetypes/articles/whichoccupationsareathighestriskofbeingautomated/2019-03-25

Office for National Statistics (ONS) (2021a) Early indicators of UK population size and age structure. 16 April. Available from https://www.ons.gov.uk/peoplepopulationandcommunity/populationandmigration/populationestimates/datasets/earlyindicatorsofukpopulationsizeandagestructure

Office for National Statistics (ONS) (2021b) Unemployment rate (aged 16 and over, seasonally adjusted). 12 October. Available from https://www.ons.gov.uk/employmentandlabourmarket/peoplenotinwork/unemployment/timeseries/mgsx/lms

Open Access Government (2020) *The FUDIPO Project: AI Systems in Process Industries.* Open Access Government. Crewe, Cheshire: Adjacent Digital Politics Ltd. Available from https://www.openaccessgovernment.org/the-fudipo-project-ai-systems-in-process-industries/83756/

PwC CB Insights (2020) MoneyTree report. San Francisco: PwC CB Insights.

Pytorch (n.d.) Available from https://pytorch.org/

Shadbolt, P. (2015) In a hurry? Let a robot valet park your car. *CNN Business.* 30 January. Available from https://edition.cnn.com/2015/01/30/tech/mci-robot-parking-valet/index.html

Shead, S. (2021) UK aims to boost solar by predicting cloud movements with A.I. *CNBC Sustainable Future.* 23 August. Available from https://www.cnbc.com/2021/08/23/uk-to-use-ex-deepmind-scientists-cloud-predicting-ai-to-boost-solar.html

Slegers, J. (2021) Ocado Group blog. 3 June. Available from https://www.ocadogroup.com/technology/blog/how-we-use-digital-twin-simulations-optimise-present-de-risk-future-and-discover

Stone, T. (2021) New UK autonomous vehicle trial begins on public roads in Birmingham. *TTI.* 10 June. Available from https://www.traffictechnologytoday.com/news/autonomous-vehicles/new-uk-autonomous-vehicle-trial-begins-on-public-roads-in-birmingham.html

Stroke Association (n.d.) Symptoms of stroke. Available from https://www.stroke.org.uk/what-is-stroke/what-are-the-symptoms-of-stroke

TechTarget (n.d.) Available from https://searchcio.techtarget.com/definition/business-innovation

TensorFlow Learn (n.d.) Available from https://www.tensorflow.org/

The Future of Life Institute (2017) Asilomar AI principles. Available from https://futureoflife.org/ai-principles/

UK Government (2019) *Policy Paper – AI Sector Deal.* London: UK Government.

UK Government (2020) Guidance – Trend Deck 2021: Skills, June. Available from https://www.gov.uk/government/publications/trend-deck-2021-skills/trend-deck-2021-skills

United Nations (n.d.) Sustainable development goals. Available from https://www.un.org/sustainabledevelopment/

US Bureau of Labor Statistics (2021) Civilian unemployment rate. Available from https://www.bls.gov/charts/employment-situation/civilian-unemployment-rate.htm

Williams, R. (2019) Fan Hui: What I learned from losing to DeepMind's AlphaGo. *i.* 25 May. Available from https://inews.co.uk/news/technology/fan-hui-what-i-learned-from-losing-to-deepminds-alphago-google-295005

FURTHER READING

Bornet, P., Barkin, I. and Wirtz, J. (2020) *Intelligent Automation – Welcome to the World of HYPERAUTOMATION.* Published by the authors.

Burgess, A. (2018) *The Executive Guide to Artificial Intelligence: How to Identify and Implement Applications for AI in your Organisation.* Cham: Palgrave Macmillan.

Crawford, K. (2021) The *Atlas of AI: Power, Politics, and the Planetary Costs of Artificial Intelligence.* Newhaven, US: Yale University Press.

Willcocks, L. P. and Lacity, M. C. (2016) *Service Automation, Robots and the Future of Work.* Stratford upon Avon: Steve Brooks Publishing.

Willcocks, L. P. and Lacity, M. C. (2018) *Robotic Process and Cognitive Automation, The Next Phase.* Stratford upon Avon: Steve Brooks Publishing.

Willcocks, L. P., Hindle, J. and Lacity, M. C. (2019) *Becoming Strategic with Robotic Process Automation.* Stratford upon Avon: Steve Brooks Publishing.

Wooldridge, M. (2020) *The Road to Conscious Machines: The Story of AI.* London: Pelican Books.

INDEX

Page numbers in italics refer to figures and tables.

reduced contact 12

'ReLu' (Rectified Linear Unit) 29

RESTful application programming interfaces (REST APIs) 80

return on investment (RoI) 10

revolutionary operating models 8

risks 6, 24, 33, 36, 67, 69, 71, 72, 73, 108, 112, 113, 118, 123, 125, 128 127, 129

  mitigation of 61, 126, 127, 128

robotic desktop automation (RDA) see robotic process automation

robotic process automation (RPA) 10, 13, 48, 58, 59, 60, 64–6, 66, 67, 68, 71, 73, 79, 80, 82, 120

root cause analysis 50

Royal Berkshire NHS Foundation Trust (RBFT) 56, 92–8, 112, 113, 128

sales optimisation 100

self-service 12, 17, 46, 79, 85, 88, 112, 115, 124

sentiment 4, 25, 62, 63, 80, 114

service level agreements (SLAs) 80

'shadow IT' 118

shared services 11, 12, 78

shared services concepts (SSCs) 11

Siemens Global Business Services 32, 59, 77–82, 111, 112

Six Sigma 11, 15

skilled work 123, 125

skill shortage 8, 122, 123

skill-shortage vacancies (SSVs) 122, 123

social impact 26

social media 10, 72, 87, 114, 125, 129

software

  accounting 5, 12

  AI-enabled 5, 64, 92

  CRM 4

  development 19, 24, 127

enterprise resource planning (ERP) 50, 110

facial recognition 126

IDP 19

intelligent 4, 6, 58

licences 12

non-intelligent 4, 15

outdated 117

platforms 12

poor development 127

process mining 6, 15, 68

procurement 5

robotic process automation (RPA) 10, 58, 64, 65

robots 35, 55, 59, 60, 65, 110, 111

sales optimisation 100

solutions 11, 48, 58, 62, 64, 67, 110

task mining 68, 69

tools 22, 67, 109–10, 127

vendor 19, 50, 65, 66, 67, 98, 117

specific function toolkits 23, 25, 27, 34–5

speech recognition 25, 63

staff training 118

start-ups 3, 8, 9, 18, 19

statistical analysis 11, 69

strategic decisions 6, 108

structured data 4, 15, 58, 60, 62, 64, 80

system failure 50, 69, 110

task mining 24, 60, 67, 68–9

technology platform 3, 19

technology shift 42

Tensorflow 11, 36

Tesla 8

text mining 80

Thrombectomy Innovation and Transformation Network (TITAN) 92

tone 4, 5, 33, 37

toolkits 5, 21, 22, 26, 30, 31, 35, 36, 38, 40, 54

business function 22, 23, 24, 32–4, 69, 82

configurable 23–4, 23 32

optimal use of 31

specific function 23, 25, 27, 34–5

technology 23

types of 23, 32–5

virtual assistant 50

tracking 128

training data 27, 28, 29, 30, 31, 126

transactional process automation 3, 4, 58

Twitter 126

Uber 8, 10, 42

unattended automation 65, 66 see also RPA

unemployment rate 124, 124, 125, 125

unstructured data 4, 5, 15, 36, 58, 62, 65, 80

UN sustainable development goals 128

user interface 22, 23, 32, 33, 45, 58, 64, 117

vendors 21, 24, 27, 31, 66, 127

  application 23, 35

  IA 10, 59

  NLP 127

  platform 35, 82

  RPA 59, 65

  software 19, 50, 65, 66, 67, 98, 117

  strategy 37, 38

  technology 18, 128

VIRA (Virtual, Interactive, Responsive Assistant) 85–9, 112, 113, 114

virtual agents 24, 33, 36

virtual models 6, 108

Wärtsilä 56, 99–103, 113